THE DYESS STORY

THE DYESS STORY

THE DYESS STORY

The Eye-Witness Account of the
DEATH MARCH FROM BATAAN
and the Narrative of Experiences
in Japanese Prison Camps and
of Eventual Escape

BY

LT. COL. WM. E. DYESS

Edited, with a biographical introduction, by

CHARLES LEAVELLE

G·P·PUTNAM'S SONS
NEW YORK

TO THE AMERICAN HEROES OF THE PHILIPPINES—
LIVING AND DEAD—AND THEIR GALLANT FILIPINO
COMRADES, THIS BOOK IS HUMBLY DEDICATED.

This book is based upon a series of stories first published by *The Chicago Tribune,* whose kindness in permitting their reproduction here is gratefully acknowledged, and special thanks should be given to Melvin H. Wagner of the *Tribune,* who drew the maps, and to Swain Scalf, also of the *Tribune,* who took, both at White Sulphur Springs and Champaign, the photographs here reproduced which are not otherwise credited.

ILLUSTRATIONS

The illustrations will be found between pages 96 and 97.

7

INTRODUCTION

IN THE HUMID HEAT of an Australian field hospital on a day in July, 1942, the late Byron Darnton of *The New York Times* was talking to Lieutenant (now Major) Ben S. Brown, fighter pilot of the United States Army Air Forces. Brown, awaiting a minor operation, had been one of the last American officers to be evacuated from the Philippines before the fall of Bataan.

"I didn't want you to come to see me so I could talk about myself," Brown was saying. "I want to tell you about Captain Ed Dyess. I don't think his story has been told back in the United States and I think it ought to be. Ed is a Texas boy, over six feet tall. He was twenty-six years old this month. Boy! Was he the ideal officer!"

Brown talked on and Darnton took notes, though the story already was more than three months old. The dispatch he sent was printed throughout the country, then it was clipped out and buried with a million other items in newspaper morgues. Darnton was killed three months later in an airplane crash somewhere in New Guinea.

But the stage had been set for one of the most dramatic news breaks of the war. Nineteen months later, in January, 1944, the Dyess story burst upon a shocked nation. It was acclaimed by statesmen, clergymen, editors, and the American people as an historic document which would figure decisively in the shaping of peace terms for Japan; one whose full significance could be measured by time alone.

The story of Dyess and his companions and the atrocities they had witnessed had been withheld for months by the government in the fear that its publication would result in death to thousands of American prisoners still in Japanese hands. When all hope of aiding the prisoners passed, the story was released.

The swift recognition of the Dyess story's importance is due largely to Byron Darnton's dispatch, which might never have been written, except that World War II has been the most fully reported conflict in history. The army of newspaper and magazine correspondents and photographers is the greatest ever assigned to a war. Their intensive coverage of even the most remote sectors on the battlefronts of the world has unearthed and preserved thrilling and historical chapters by the thousands. It was this new standard of war reporting that took Darnton to the isolated Australian hospital where he met Ben Brown.

It was a year later, in July, 1943, that a brief telegraphic dispatch chronicled the safety and good health of one Major William Edwin Dyess, of the army air forces, who for many months had been a prisoner of the Imperial Japanese army. In some newspapers the dispatch appeared as written. In many others it did not appear. Certain editors sent the dispatch to their morgues with the scribbled query: "Who is he?" And when the Darnton clipping was laid before them, the Dyess item became big news.

"Ed was the commanding officer of the field squadron," the *Times* correspondent had written in the words of Lieutenant Brown. "Ed had a lot of work to do, but nine times out of ten when a dangerous mission came up he would take it. There wasn't anything the pilots wouldn't do for Ed, because he never asked them to do what he wouldn't do.

"We got word one day that three 12,000-ton tankers and transports, a cruiser, and some destroyers had pulled into Subic bay on the western coast of Luzon island. Ed took a P-40, hung a 500-pound bomb onto its belly, and started out to bomb and strafe the Japs. He made three trips. I was his relief pilot, but he wouldn't let me fly. He did it all himself.

"He missed the ships with this bomb but hit a small island on which supplies were stored and blew them up. By strafing, he blew up one 12,000-ton ship, beached another, and sank two 100-ton launches. And he strafed troops and docks and caused a lot of casualties.

"Next day the Japanese radio reported that Subic bay had

been attacked by a big force of four-engined bombers and forty or fifty fighters. I tell you that to give you an idea of the sort of guy Ed is.

"The time came when we had to get out of Bataan. We had only a few planes left and the jig was up. Ed gave orders for all of his pilots to leave. But he refused to go himself.

"There were 175 men and 25 officers who could not possibly get away because there was nothing to take them away in. And Ed wouldn't go unless they could. I tried to get him to, but he wouldn't."

Dyess's importance as an American hero—as established by Darnton's dispatch—was responsible for a concerted rush to obtain the full story. And when, in the course of their efforts, newspapers and magazine editors learned something of Dyess's appalling experiences in Japanese prison camps, the struggle for the right to publish them grew epochal.

By September 5, 1943, when Dyess was recuperating in the army's Ashford General Hospital at White Sulphur Springs, West Virginia, the stiffening competition had narrowed the field of bidders to a national weekly magazine and *The Chicago Tribune,* representing 100 associated newspapers. The *Tribune* was successful, not because it outbid the magazine, but because it could promise Dyess, now a lieutenant colonel, a daily circulation of ten million and an estimated daily audience of forty million against the magazine's circulation of about three million weekly and estimated reader audience of twelve million. Colonel Dyess's consuming determination to expose to the world Japan's barbaric trea·e ment of American war prisoners decided him in favor of th-daily newspapers and their vastly larger audience.   ne

The *Tribune* obtained the War Department's permissi for Colonel Dyess to tell his story. Only three days later ý to retary of War withdrew the permission and forbade D hile to divulge any further details of his prison camp experier ear or escape from the Japs. The *Tribune* had the story, but ve faced a four-and-a-half-month battle for its release. Officer-reluctance, indecision, resistance, and actual hostility in Hove places all contributed to lengthening the fight. In the ç the

the story came out and was given to the American people by their newspapers.

There was good reason in July, 1943, why editors might have been slow to recognize the Dyess epic for what it was. In the first place, Dyess himself was practically unknown. Many editors, as has been seen, lacked the background material that would have established him as a hero of the first rank. At that time, too, the Swedish repatriation liner *Gripsholm* already had made one trip, returning American civilian internees who had flooded the magazines and newspapers with stories of Jap callousness and neglect. Japanese prison stories were on their way to being old stuff. But to those who read it, the Darnton dispatch carried a mighty message: here was a man who had lived behind the curtain of military secrecy the Japanese had drawn upon Bataan after the surrender and who could tell what actually had happened to the battered remnants of MacArthur's armies after the Stars and Stripes had been hauled down.

It was on one of those perfect fall mornings the West Virginia mountain country knows so well that I first met Ed Dyess. He was pale and lean to the point of spareness. His blond hair was thinning on top, though he was only twenty-seven years old. This, I was to learn, came of the barbaric Japanese sun cure to which the prisoners of Bataan had been subjected.

Heroes seldom appear heroic in hospital beds, but even so it was difficult of belief that this smiling young fellow had ken all the tortures the Japs could inflict upon him for arly a year and was the holder of the Distinguished Service ross with oak leaf cluster, the Legion of Merit, the Silver rell and the group citation award with two oak leaf clusters. there was a certain ruggedness of feature, a cold blue of on eye, and an unmistakable authority in the voice, despite in easy, Texas drawl. said Dyess was slow of speech, but every word counted, it andloped as our conversations got under way. His talk was red by pungent colloquialisms, richly descriptive. There

12

was an undercurrent of the refreshing humor that seems to be the birthright of Westerners and Southwesterners.

This young Texan seemed to be of the same breed as those slow-spoken and hard-riding Southern lads who left their homes in 1861 to follow Stonewall Jackson and Nathan Bedford Forrest. And, it turned out, he was descended—on both sides of the family—from men who had worn the gray of the Confederacy. Somehow, this raised an old question that has produced a thousand answers; what goes into the making of a hero?

On America's far-flung fighting fronts there are thousands of men who, like Colonel Dyess, measure up as the ideal American officer and fighting man. What factors go into building the self-reliant spirit, the strength of character, and the daring that make certain men outstanding, even in a fighting force conceded to be the world's best?

Is it their upbringing? Their background of life in a free America? Or is it heredity? Most authorities regard military training as a lesser factor. Military training can bring out qualities that in some men have lain dormant, but it cannot instill a quality that is not there. A study of Ed Dyess's life and background indicates that all the factors suggested here played a part in making him the hero he became.

To begin with heredity, the first Dyess in America was John, a native of Wales, who settled in Georgia as a member of the Oglethorpe colony in 1733. He was Edwin's great-great-grandfather. The flier's great-grandfather, also a John Dyess, was a Georgia planter and helped drive the Seminole Indians into the Everglades. John George Dyess, Ed's grandfather, also was a native of Georgia and a soldier in the Confederate army in the War between the States.

Colonel Dyess was not the first member of the family to be a prisoner of war. The grandfather was captured while scouting the Union lines in Pennsylvania and was held near Chicago. He refused an offer of parole because it would have compelled him to swear not to bear arms again. Shortly afterward Grandfather Dyess put a gunpowder bomb in the stove that warmed the officers' barracks. The blast shattered the stove and blew out all the windows. Because no one was injured the Southerner's only punishment was solitary confinement.

This suited his purpose admirably. A few days later he landed a haymaker on the chin of his single guard, took the guard's rifle, and escaped to the South, where he rejoined the army of General Joseph E. Johnston and fought until the end of the war.

Judge Dyess, the colonel's father, has—by his own statement—two of the most important qualifications for being President of the United States: he was born in a log cabin and went west in an ox-drawn covered wagon. This journey was from his birthplace near Alexandria, Louisiana, to west Texas.

Judge Dyess was graduated from old Burleson college, Greenville, Texas, and attended Baylor university and John Tarleton college, preparing himself for teaching. His first job was one no one else wanted. The high spirited "scholars" of Hunt county had run two teachers out of the county. The board was seeking a high spirited teacher and offered sixty-five dollars a month instead of the usual forty dollars.

Dyess, the new teacher, moved in, took some of the starch out of the most troublesome scholars, and finished the term without incident. When he accepted a better job in Shackelford county he met and married Miss Hallie Graham, a native of Oglesby, Texas. In 1914 he was elected county tax assessor, serving two terms. He was elected county judge in 1918 and held the post ten years. Since 1928 he has been district school tax assessor-collector.

Mrs. Dyess's father was Emmett Graham of Missouri, who moved to Texas during the Civil War. Her grandfather, Noah, a Confederate soldier, died in battle.

Albany, the community in which Colonel Dyess grew up, is a typical west Texas county seat and cow town. Farmers of the western and southern regions of Shackelford county trade in Stamford and Abilene, but the ranchers and punchers congregate in Albany. These men with their big hats and jingling spurs are as much a part of the town as the three-story stone

courthouse which stands in its windswept square, amid mes-
quite and cedar trees.

On the Main street side is a bronze tablet, surmounted by
a steer's head, erected "In Memory of the Texas Cattle Trail
to Dodge City and Other Northern Points: 1875-1890." Main
street, which curves in from the east and swings southward
to cross the railroad, was part of the trail.

Near-by is another tablet, at the base of a miniature oil
derrick. This slab is inscribed, "Commemorating the first
producing oil well in west Texas; completed in 1919."

It was in this town that Edwin grew up. When he still was
a youngster he joined the Boy Scouts. He could not, however, attend the weekly meetings and work. But he could
always take time off from his work to attend the carnival
which had a long stay in Albany. Once when Ed brought
home a report card that showed him low in deportment and
in grades Judge Dyess took him into the front bedroom. After
the judge had had his say the son said:

"It's all right, Dad. I will not need that when I grow up.
I'm going to be in the carnival."

Meanwhile the youngster delivered and sold a Fort Worth
newspaper. Later he worked for a filling station for eighty
dollars a month, but he put the money into the First National Bank and received his spending money from home as
usual.

It was at this time also that Edwin began slipping away to
take a few lessons from the barnstorming pilots who continued to visit Albany. It was while working on the Humble
pipeline that he met a young fellow who had just been
"washed out" at Randolph field.

Edwin had attended John Tarleton college, at Stephen-
ville, Texas, with the idea of becoming a lawyer. During his
summer vacation he had gone to enroll at the University of
Texas. But when he met the washout from Randolph field he
determined to become a flier.

Judge Dyess always had wanted Edwin to be an aviator;
both had been thrilled by Lindbergh's historic New York-
Paris flight in 1927. And the judge and his son had taken

15

their first airplane ride together in a barnstormer's rickety plane in 1920, when Ed was four years old. So, when the son went home and announced to his father in the front bedroom that he wanted an appointment to the West Point of the air the judge said:

"Son, if she can be got we'll get her."

Ed got the appointment. He arrived at San Antonio and reported at the airfield. And here is where he began to accumulate the philosophy that carried him through the Japanese prison camps. In his early days at Randolph one of his best friends was killed in an accident.

Ed saw the body. He refused to believe his pal was dead. He preferred to think of him as having been transferred to another airfield. Later, witnessing the fall of Bataan, Ed Dyess projected his philosophy. He thought of the Philippines as having been only temporarily lost. He was sure they would be regained—as they will be—and took comfort.

Ed was graduated from Kelly field, which is near Randolph. With his reserve commission as second lieutenant he was transferred to Barksdale field, Shreveport, Louisiana, as a member of the 20th Pursuit Group. When he was transferred a second time, to Hamilton field, California, he was promoted to first lieutenant and placed in command of the 21st Pursuit Squadron.

It was during his stay in California that Ed met and became engaged to Marajen Stevick, co-publisher with her mother of the Champaign (Ill.) *News-Gazette*. They were married shortly before he sailed with his squadron for Manila.

Ed's last visit home, before he went overseas, was in May, 1941. The next the folks heard of Ed he was a prisoner of war.

Shortly after this it was announced at Washington that nothing could be done for the American fighting men who had been captured. Judge Dyess and his fellow townsmen refused to take this sitting down. "There's one sure way we can go in there and get Ed," the judge told a group of Albany men who had pledged themselves to back him in anything he wanted to do. "If we can get us a submarine and somebody to run it, we can save Ed and his friends! I'm going to write General MacArthur."

And he did! The general replied that the plan was a good one, but that there were many difficulties. Judge Dyess made one more effort. He tried to ship out from one of the Texas ports in the hope that some workable plan might be developed if he could but reach the Pacific theater of war. His age, however, blocked this venture. Judge Dyess's determination in the face of a hopeless odds is mentioned as a parallel to his son's refusal to leave his junior officers and men who were to stay behind facing overwhelming odds on Bataan.

My efforts to extract from Ed Dyess a more detailed account of this decision met with little success. The point was one of the two snags encountered in the conversations at White Sulphur Springs. The other, on which he yielded after prolonged questioning, involved the detailed story of the Subic bay raid, described briefly to Darnton by Ben Brown. Dyess's objection was that a more complete account would require too much first person narrative. Later, after glancing through a rough draft of the Subic bay chapter, Ed said, "Tst, tst!" and shook his head. He added: "You sure must have a strong 'I' key on this typewriter. It's a wonder to me it didn't break down somewhere along here."

But he was not reluctant to describe in full his personal experiences on the Death March and in the prison camps. This was because the sufferings he endured were typical of those visited upon thousands of other Americans. They were definitely a part of the story he wanted the world to know.

"If you triple my troubles and multiply the result by several thousand, you'll get a rough idea of what went on," Dyess remarked at the end of the story. "And when you do that, you must bear in mind that I got out alive. Thousands of the boys didn't—and won't."

When Ed Dyess was discharged from the hospital in late September, he was entering his last three months of life. And he was under restrictions which, to many another man, might have been unbearable. He could give the press no news of himself—news thousands of Americans were waiting to hear. It was known in many army posts that Colonel Dyess had returned to the United States, yet he had to adopt a vague and formal style in replying to the hundreds of letters that reached him.

When Colonel and Mrs. Dyess went to visit her mother in Champaign, Illinois, they slipped into town and during the daylight hours remained inside the big house on Armory street. Their presence was not chronicled by Mrs. Dyess's Champaign *News-Gazette*. Though he was a national hero, Colonel Dyess remained in effect a military secret. Yet it was not this that irked him most. His great concern was his story; his abiding hope was that it be told in time to help those American fighting men still in the Japanese prisons and to arouse the people to a more determined prosecution of the war in the Pacific.

Meanwhile, the Dyess story had been written and the agreed price paid over. Colonel Dyess deposited it in a special account and never drew upon it. "If the story isn't released, I don't want anything," he said. "Money isn't important. It's the story that matters."

Colonel Dyess felt that the information he had brought back was the property of the people, and he accepted payment for it only that he might make substantial contributions to Army Air Force relief funds and the American Red Cross and assist certain of the men who were with him on Bataan, in the prison camps, and during the escape from the Japanese.

In furtherance of Colonel Dyess's hope that his contributions be sizable, the *Tribune* and associated newspapers published the Dyess story without financial profit to themselves. The *Tribune* negotiated the sale of the book in order that the fund might not be reduced by the payment of fees to an agent. In harmony with this policy, G. P. Putnam's Sons, to whom the manuscript was awarded, paid top royalties for the right of publication. The Colonel's wishes are being carried out by Mrs. Dyess, to whom he confided them in detail.

As the Champaign visit drew to a close, Colonel Dyess was

notified that upon expiration of his leave he would report for duty with the 4th Air Force, on the west coast. En route there he paid a visit—long delayed—to his home town of Albany. The entire community turned out two thousand strong. The news spread across the range country, and there was an inrush of booted and sombreroed ranch owners and their punchers. When the press wires carried a story that Colonel Dyess would address a gathering of home folk the night following his return, a perturbed press relations officer telephoned from Washington. But the celebration went on as planned. Ed Dyess disclosed nothing of his secret—even to his parents. He proposed that the welcome be dedicated to those Americans still in Jap prisons. The throng stood to applaud many minutes as Ed took his place behind the microphone, alternately gulping and smiling in the glare of floodlights. Then he said he felt as though he had swallowed a ten-gallon hat that would go down just so far and no farther. He paid tribute to the Hereford beefsteaks of Shackelford county, contrasting them with the carabao meat of Bataan. "You put a rock in the cooking pot with the meat and when the rock melts the carabao is tender." He said that Tojo's boys were on the run and that buying war bonds would keep 'em running. Then he shook hands with everybody and that ended the homecoming.

A few weeks later, Colonel Dyess returned to duty, flying a P-38 Lightning—a two-engined fighter whose dazzling speed always had fascinated him.

Until the end he insisted that he be kept informed of each step in the campaign to win release of his story. He probably was the only one who never seemed discouraged by the repeated turndowns. His premise was a simple one: that his disclosures were too momentous, his story too big to remain long suppressed. He foresaw grave repercussions for the suppressors and was convinced that in time they too would see the light.

Colonel Dyess did not live to see the proof of his premise. It was five weeks to the day after he had crashed to his death in Burbank, California, that tall type in a hundred news-

19

papers from coast to coast heralded the start of "DYESS'S OWN STORY!" Nor did he live to learn that he had been recommended for the highest military award his government can bestow: the Congressional Medal of Honor. This was announced to Judge and Mrs. Dyess and the townsfolk by Brigadier General Russell E. Randall, commanding the 4th Air Force, as they stood in Albany's windswept cemetery on December 27. Mrs. Dyess had gently insisted that her son be laid to rest near his boyhood home, rather than in Arlington National Cemetery as had been proposed.

That the Dyess story stirred the nation more deeply probably than any event since Pearl Harbor, there can be little doubt. This was evidenced by tremendous reader response recorded in the hundred newspapers that gave it to the people and by the concerted demand upon Congress to strengthen our forces in the Pacific. On January 27, the day a joint army-navy statement gave a generalization of the disclosures to come, Secretary of State Hull addressed a blunt warning to Japan. Those responsible for the crimes against American prisoners of war will be made to pay in full, he said. Secretary Hull mentioned specific crimes and named the victims, quoting from Colonel Dyess's official report of what he had seen. Without question, the story he was spared to tell will be the means of avenging his comrades who were not spared and, equally important, will speed the day of vengeance.

CHARLES LEAVELLE.

THE DYESS STORY

CHAPTER ONE

FROM THE AFTER DECK of our transport I looked back through the Golden Gate to San Francisco's terraces of twinkling lights. I wondered what changes might come to the mellow old city and to me before I should see it again.

It was the night of November 1, 1941. We were outward bound for Manila and the Philippines. With me were thirteen pilots and a ground crew of the 21st Pursuit Squadron, United States Army Air Forces, of which I was captain and commander. The rest of our fellows were waiting near San Francisco, expecting sailing orders within a few days. Also on board were pilots and technicians of the 34th Pursuit Squadron, commanded by First Lieutenant Samuel Maratt.

Both groups had been shipped out in a hurry, without planes. New ships were to be ready for us at Nichols field, our destination. But as the transport slid through the starlit night, I wondered if there would be a Nichols field when we got there.

I should explain that for weeks we all had been convinced that war with Japan was imminent. Nor was our conviction shaken by the quiet ribbings handed us by our civilian friends.

We were to remember their laughter in the weeks that followed. It reflected the attitude of the nation. It was explanation, in a measure, of America's bewilderment and shock at the bombing of Pearl Harbor. Yet we knew nothing the civilians didn't know. The newspapers had publicized

23

each move in that tragic chess game; the mounting tension between Washington and Tokio and the strained diplomatic correspondence between the two capitals, each note sharper and more ominous than the last. This had gone so far by November 1 that as we embarked we were impatient of even the slightest delay, lest hostilities start before our arrival at our Philippines station. We had no doubt that Manila would be Japan's first target.

The beauties of our Pacific voyage were, I am afraid, lost upon us. I have only a vague memory of those sun-drenched days and moonlit nights. But I remember clearly that we devoured every scrap of news that reached us by radio and that we chafed and made sharp comments each day when the ship's run for the preceding twenty-four hours was announced.

We disembarked at Manila on November 20 and were relieved to learn there still was no war. At Nichols field we were gratified to find preparations proceeding at a furious pace. It was obvious at once that we were facing a colossal task, and with each day's developments the international situation grew more explosive.

On November 26 the United States warned Japan to get out of the Axis and out of China and to cease all aggression. Tokio responded bluntly that it could not comply.

A few days later, Japan massed troops on Thailand's borders in the face of warnings by President Roosevelt. The government shut off shipment of American oil to Japan and froze Japanese credits in the United States. Simultaneously, we began speeding troops and material to the Philippines. How anything short of war could have been expected I do not know.

The story I am about to tell covers the twenty months between our arrival in the Philippines and my return to the United States. In the telling I hope I can picture with lasting realism the selfless courage of those thousands—those few thousands—of American and Filipino fighting men who held the Philippines against the fury of the Japanese for four long months.

I want to picture in stark detail the barbaric cruelties inflicted upon the survivors in a succession of Japanese prison camps; the horrors of hunger and thirst, of sickness and neglect, and of a daily existence in which the sight and stench of death were ever present.

But even more terrible than the prison camp sufferings was the barbaric Death March from Bataan, an 85-mile trek from Mariveles, Bataan province, to San Fernando, Pampanga, under the merciless tropical sun. It began on April 10, 1942, the day after our surrender. The wanton murder, by beheadal, of an American army captain as the march was getting under way symbolized the horrors that were to come.

In the days that followed I saw the Japs plunge bayonets into malaria-stricken American and Filipino soldiers who were struggling to keep their feet as they were herded down the dusty roads that led to hell. I saw an American colonel flogged until his face was unrecognizable.

I saw laughing and yelling Jap soldiers lean from speeding trucks to smash their rifle butts against the heads of the straggling prisoners.

I saw Jap soldiers roll unconscious American and Filipino prisoners of war into the path of the Japanese army trucks which ran over them.

I saw and experienced for the first time the infamous Japanese sun cure, which can break a strong man. Thousands of American and Filipino war prisoners, mostly bareheaded, were forced at noonday, when the tropical sun was at the zenith, to sit in its direct rays until the sturdiest of us thought we must give up and until hundreds of our sick and weakened comrades did give up to delirium and death.

And it was on this march of death that most of us went practically without food for six days, others for twelve days, and all of us without water except for a few sips dipped from vile carabao wallows.

I am going to describe in detail the daily life, the misery and torture that characterized the 361 days I existed in three prison camps and a prison ship; a period of starvation and horror that took the lives of about 6,000 American and many

25

thousands more Filipino war prisoners out of a total of 50,000 men who started from Bataan. Finally, I will tell how a few of us escaped.

But what I want you really to understand and to ponder upon is the truth of what happened to America's fighting men and their brave Filipino comrades after the Stars and Stripes had been hauled down on the battlefields of Bataan.

I told my story first to General Douglas MacArthur in his Southwest Pacific headquarters last summer. When I had finished he shook my hand and congratulated me on our escape. Then he added:

"It is a story that should be told to the American people. But I am afraid, Captain, that the people back home will find it hard to believe you. I believe you. Make no mistake about that. I know the Japs."

A few nights later, after a swift passage through the far-flung Pacific theater of war, I looked again upon the lights of San Francisco. Even from a height of 5,000 feet it was plain that changes had come to the old city since that night in November, 1941. The lights that had twinkled against the rising background of hills now were shrouded and dimmed, or had disappeared.

With the deep-throated roar of the bomber's four motors filling my ears, I wondered drowsily what changes the last twenty months had wrought in me. As we dropped in for our landing I concluded that time alone can reveal their full extent.

Before the week was out I reported to my commanding officers in the War Department at Washington, D. C. I told my story. For more than three hours they listened in taut silence. At its conclusion they said:

"It is one of the most momentous stories of the war. It is one the American people must know. But do you think they can grasp its enormity? Do you think they can credit it?"

I said I didn't know. I remembered all too well that there had been times during the Death March from Bataan and in the prison camps that I could scarcely credit the testimony of my own eyes and ears. I told my superiors our people simply must believe this account of atrocity, unparalleled since the Indian wars of our Colonial days.

With military thoroughness they set about corroborating what I had told them. They interrogated my companions and consulted independent sources. And they were successful; appallingly so. Here, then, is my story.

My first feeling of being actually at war with Japan came to me during a dramatic fifteen minutes in group headquarters at Nichols field on December 6, 1941. This was two days before the Pearl Harbor raid, which for us was on December 8, Far Eastern time.

It was midmorning, and we were summoned to headquarters by the late Brigadier General Harold H. George, then colonel and our chief air officer. He looked at us in somber silence as we walked into the long room and sat down on benches and chairs.

He was not a tall man and the breadth of his shoulders made him appear shorter. He stood with arms folded and looked into each of our faces in turn. Then he spoke:

"Men," he said, "you are not a suicide squadron yet, but you're damned close to it. There will be war with Japan in a very few days. It may come in a matter of hours."

We sat tensely expectant. From outside the building came the distant drone of motors on the testing blocks. Within, there was no sound except our commander's voice.

"The Japs have a minimum of 3,000 planes they can send down on us from Formosa [600 miles to the north] and from aircraft carriers," he went on. "They know the way already. When they come again they will be tossing something."

We had already had a hint of this. For several nights Jap planes had been flying over Luzon and other islands of the Philippines group. Our planes actually had gone up to intercept the Japs but had failed because our inadequate air warning service had not functioned rapidly enough.

Colonel George then gave us his carefully prepared estimate of the number of planes necessary to defend the islands against such a Jap force. We were shocked.

"Yes," he concluded, "you men know how many planes we can put into the air. Well, that's the job you will be facing within a very short time."

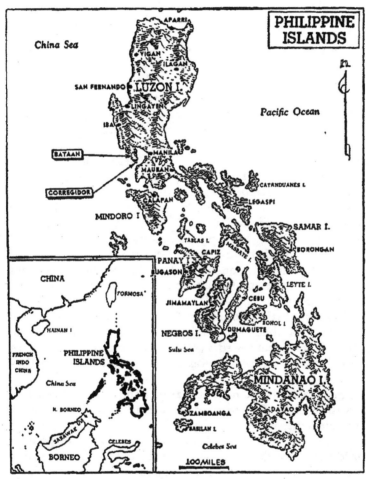

No one doubted the truth and seriousness of the situation as we walked back to the hangars where we had been working furiously to get our available planes into fighting shape. On arrival, my squadron was issued some well-worn P-35s. We flew these until December 4, then turned them over to the 34th and began receiving P-40Es, which transports were bringing in from the United States. None of the guns had been fired. We had to install and boresight them.

In boresighting, the guns are fired and adjusted until the bullets strike the spot where the sights are centered. We were handicapped in this because of the acute shortage of .50-caliber ammunition. Only a few rounds were issued for test purposes.

On the day the Japs attacked, our squadron was given four new P-40Es and I really mean new. None of them ever had been in the air. The gun barrels still were packed with cosmolene [heavy grease]. The Filipino mechanics assigned to help us prepare for eventualities were more hindrance than help. Taking a plane off after one of these lads had worked on it was sometimes a thrilling experience.

At 2:30 A.M. of December 8—with much work still to be done—we were ordered to stations for the sixth successive day. None of the eighteen planes waiting on the line had been in the air more than three hours. We could see their ghostly outlines through the open fly of the emergency operations tent where we assembled under the dim glow of a blacked out gas lantern.

There was little talk among the youngsters gathered about me. Many of them were only a few months out of flying school. Upon them rested a grave responsibility; their role in the defense of the islands was to be a major one. And they faced it like veterans.

They knew the zero hour was at hand. It had been two days since Colonel George had called it "a matter of hours." The telephone rang.

I remember well the exclamations and looks of surprise as I told them that the Japs had taken the plunge, but that they had passed us up for the moment and were bombing Pearl Harbor, thousands of miles to the east. We didn't know then, of course, about the fleet concentration the Jap bombers had chosen for a knockout blow.

We waited restlessly in the operations tent, while the sun

came up, silhouetting our gleaming new planes. At 10:30 A.M. the orders came, via the squadron radio: "Tally-ho, Clark field!" We took off immediately, fifteen planes following me up. One flight, still working on the new P-40s, got off five minutes later.

I radioed air force headquarters that we were climbing to 24,000 feet and heading for Clark, several miles northward. We were just north of Manila when we were ordered back to a point midway between Corregidor and Cavite to intercept Jap bombers. But the air was empty of enemies when we got there. The Japs had been warned and had ducked back out to sea, later striking elsewhere.

Meanwhile, the flight that had gotten off late headed for Clark field and got into the scrap there, shooting down three Jap dive bombers, but were unable to stop the intensive bombing that left the field in ruins. We saw them again at Nichols field that afternoon while our planes were being serviced. Lieutenant Sam Grashio's plane had a wing hole you could throw a hat through.

"By God," said Sam. "They ain't shootin' spitballs, are they?"

Orders now came for abandonment of Nichols field. It was too exposed. It was late afternoon when we took off in beautiful flying weather for Clark field, our new base. There were almost no clouds. Across the blue of Manila bay stood the mountains of Bataan, clear and sharp in the brilliant sunshine.

At 4,000 feet we could see the towering pillars of smoke that marked our destination. We were over Clark field after a few minutes of flight. It was a mess. Oil dumps and hangars were blazing fiercely. Planes were burning on the ground. Runways had been bombed so systematically we could use only the auxiliary landing strip. This was little better than a country road.

Each landing stirred up blinding dust clouds. We could go down only at intervals of several minutes. The sun had set and the tropical dusk had deepened into darkness when the last planes landed in the eerie glow cast by the smoldering

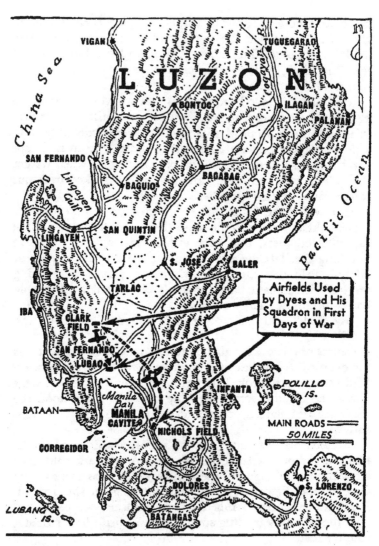

The map shows LUZON, with locations including VIGAN, TUGUEGARAO, BONTOC, ILAGAN, PALANAN, SAN FERNANDO, BAGABAG, BAGUIO, SAN QUINTIN, LINGAYEN, S. JOSE, BALER, TARLAC, IBA, CLARK FIELD, SAN FERNANDO, LUBAO, INFANTA, POLILLO IS., BATAAN, MANILA, CAVITE, CORREGIDOR, NICHOLS FIELD, DOLORES, S. LORENZO, LUBANG IS., BATANGAS. Bodies of water: China Sea, Lingayen Gulf, Manila Bay, Pacific Ocean, Cagayan R.

Airfields Used by Dyess and His Squadron in First Days of War

MAIN ROADS ========
50 MILES

hangars. It was a job to weave the planes in and out among
the bomb craters.

After a search, we found group headquarters, which had
been moved into the jungle at the edge of the field. We slept

that night on the floor of a dugout, after a dinner of cold canned beans, blackberry jam, bread, and cold coffee.

We were off at dawn to intercept bombers reported heading our way. Two planes cracked up on the bomb-pocked field, and Lieutenant Robert D. Clark, of Cleveland, O., was killed. The bombers never showed up.

We learned that day what it's like to fly for hours at 15,000 feet and above without oxygen. There was none at Clark field. Without it, that night found me so done in I doubt I could have seen a Jap even if he had been in the cockpit with me.

Late the following morning I met my first Jap in the air. My tracers showed that I raked him from nose to tail. I was so busy watching two others above me that I never saw what became of the Jap I hit. But the fight pepped me up.

I landed and went to the temporary mess near our jungle headquarters to get some lunch. The late Lieutenant (later Colonel) Boyd D. (Buzz) Wagner and I were in the midst of our meal when we were warned at 12:28 P.M. that Jap bombers were heading for us and would be overhead at 12:30. This was about as much warning as we ever got, incidentally.

I dropped my food and ran to the edge of the field just as a motorcycle dispatch bearer chugged up. I jumped on the luggage carrier and told him to hightail it for the line. I didn't see Buzz anywhere and wondered how he would get to his plane in time. My next meeting with him was a shock to us both. When we reached the line I jumped off the motorcycle and into my ship.

I was halfway through the takeoff run in an opaque dust cloud before I realized I had left goggles, helmet, and parachute behind. But it was too late then. I missed the bomb craters and got into the air, flying absolutely blind in the pall left by the other planes.

When I shot out of the dust, into the dazzling sunlight, I almost jumped out of the cockpit. Right beside me was another P-40, its wing tip almost touching mine. The other pilot appeared equally startled. Then I saw it was Buzz. He recognized me at the same time. He laughed like a hyena. I

32

laughed, too—rather shakily, I think—then we pulled apart.

The radio now informed us the bombers had chosen the Manila waterfront instead of Clark field. I headed in that direction and soon saw them, dropping their eggs along the already battered shipping centers. I was almost there before I pressed the trigger to warm up my guns. Nothing happened. I tried again and was rewarded only by a discouraging click. I was getting very close now.

I radioed for the 34th Squadron to take off in the P-35s, then tried the guns a third time. All were useless. This was beyond understanding. They had worked perfectly during the morning fight.

There was nothing to do but head for Mother Earth. I landed in a small auxiliary field north of Manila. There three American soldiers helped me charge the guns [force cartridges into the firing chambers] with a screwdriver. But it was too late. When I got back over Manila the Japs had done their work and were gone, leaving a rolling smoke cloud along the waterfront.

During the next two days the Japs began landing operations at Vigan and Lingayen gulf in northern Luzon and we were sent to give them a taste of concentrated .50-caliber fire. This was in support of General MacArthur's strategy of harassing the Jap columns which were advancing from the south and counterattacking while withdrawing his own weary troops to the north. Our part was to strafe wherever needed.

At Lingayen gulf the 34th Squadron lost its commander. Lieutenant Maratt, who had run up a nice score against the Jap landing barges, tackled a big power boat. He came in low, letting it have everything six .50-caliber machine guns could deliver. He literally knocked it to pieces. Then, as he was passing directly above it, the gasoline tanks exploded, catching his plane in the pillar of flame and wreckage. This action was our last from Clark field.

I reorganized my squadron and pooled what remained of the aircraft. My ground crew, left at Nichols field the first day of the war, was with me again.

We had been ordered to a new field that was being laid

out near Lubao, about fifty air miles northwest of Manila, in Pampanga province. The Japs were advancing steadily, despite General MacArthur's delaying action, and in the weeks that followed we gave up field after field, retiring to new ones farther away.

Lubao field supposedly was completed, but when I went ahead of the squadron to verify this I found the runway still under construction. There were no ground installations and no revetments for the planes. I stayed there, taking charge of the 300 Filipino laborers and working them in shifts twenty-four hours a day.

On Christmas eve our twenty-six remaining planes arrived; twenty-five P-40s and an A-27, which had been used both for attack and dive bombing. The first plane to come in hit a soft spot in the field, bounded into the air in a complete somersault, and hit on its nose, injuring Lieutenant Tex Marable.

The 300 Filipinos ran wildly on the field like so many chickens. They were directly in the path of the other planes which were just dropping in. It looked as if a mass tragedy was inevitable. The next I remember, I was running at them, yelling like a wild Indian and firing my automatic. The bullets were whining just over their heads. Those boys were off the field and into a cane patch in nothing flat. They didn't come back for hours.

CHAPTER TWO

CHRISTMAS DINNER OF 1941 was our last feast for many a day. The evacuation of Manila was under way and it was possible to send into the city for anything we wanted. We had roast turkey, canned cranberry sauce, and plum pudding, and plenty of vegetables and coffee. And there were a few drops of holiday cheer.

But the holiday began and ended with that dinner. The situation grew in gravity with each moment. General Mac-Arthur had quit his Manila headquarters on Christmas eve, leaving orders that declared the Philippine capital an open city on Christmas day. He now was in the field, fighting to stem the enemy tide that already was sweeping northward toward Lubao.

Our biggest job was to camouflage the field. It lay along the road over which an endless stream of trucks, artillery, and service units was retiring toward Bataan. Jap dive bombers and fighter planes blasted the highway all day long. We were in constant danger of being discovered.

Working along with Filipinos, we divided the 3,500-foot runway into halves. The first half we covered with windrows of dead cane, which looked from the air as though it had been cut and left to lie. The other section was left bare, like a newly planted field. Before a takeoff we scanned the skies for Japs, then the Filipinos removed the cane. After we had gone, they replaced it and swept the bare section clear of landing wheel tracks.

Revetments for the planes were dug into the ground at the edge of a cane field. When the planes were in, they were covered by nets of chicken wire into which were stuck stalks of fresh, green cane. In front of each plane was a row of bamboo tubes which also held green cane stalks. From the air the illusion was perfect.

During the construction period we were well guarded by anti-aircraft crews. It was our hope that if prying Jap planes should come over they would come singly or in a small group. Only one ever paid us a visit and it stayed—permanently. The visitation was just after noon of a day when I was supervising one of the last phases of the cane patch camouflage.

I heard Jap motors and saw a two-engined bomber coming toward us at 2,000 feet. He would pass directly over the field. The bomb doors were still open. We learned later the plane

35

had just blasted a bridge two miles away. One of our anti-aircraft guns opened up just across the highway. A burst partially obscured the Jap for a second, and when he came out of the smoke I could see daylight between the fuselage and the port engine. The next instant, flames burst through the open bomb doors and billowed out behind the plane, which heeled over and started down.

From where I stood it looked as though he would hit me right between the eyes. There was no use running because he was turning and twisting as he fell and might strike anywhere. When the flaming ship was within a hundred feet of the ground I started hotfooting it.

The Jap struck in the cane patch with a glorious explosion that sent flaming gasoline in every direction and set fire to the cane. He had come down among five of our ships, but none of them got a scratch. All hands turned out to extinguish the fire before other Japs could be attracted by the smoke.

The explosion had scattered maps, charts, and papers over a wide area and I set the Filipinos to gathering these up. I told them to bring me everything they might find; everything. They obeyed to the letter, one of them handing me the jawbone and big teeth of a Jap flier.

In addition to the task of camouflaging the field, we flew reconnaissance and other missions every day. On December 26, while returning from a mission with Captain Charles (Bud) Sprague we met a Jap dive bomber on his way home after an attack on our troops. I gave Bud the high sign and we started down. Just before I got within range the Jap saw me and dived. I was well into my dive, however, and soon came up with him. Just as I did so, the rear gunner put three holes in my plane. I riddled him before the pilot could twist away.

Our speed was so great that Bud and I both slid past his tail. We were just over the treetops now and the Jap could dive no farther. When he straightened out I got in a long burst and saw him take fire and go into the woods. I could see the black smoke plume for a long way on the trip home.

Two days later I met a Jap Zero pilot who was a lot smarter

and a lot tougher. I was on a reconnaissance mission in the Lingayen gulf region, with a lieutenant now a prisoner of war. He was weaving along on my tail to keep Japs off while I counted ships, barges, and truck trains, and noted troop movements.

When the mission was completed I looked back for him, but he was not there. A little later I looked again and he still seemed to be absent. Just then there was a loud boom and my plane lurched.

"Well, well," I thought. "The boy's got one right under me."

I banked and looked down. Just below and behind me was a Zero, jockeying to get in another burst. I pulled over into a dive as though I was about to spin. The Jap followed me down, ready to cut loose at the first sign of trickery. I dived a long distance—those P-40s will really do it—and put a safer distance between us. Then I zoomed, coming out behind and above him. He cut around and started up at me, head on. We both opened fire. I could see his tracers passing to the right at about the height of my head.

He shot out one of my guns and put twenty-seven holes in the right wing of the P-40 before I centered my fire and took the top off his motor. As I passed over him he burst into flames and started down. Several of the boys got their first Japs during this period.

On December 30 we had some real fun. Flying at 7,000 feet several miles east of Lingayen gulf, I spotted a truck convoy, crawling along a hilly road near Baguio. With me was my companion of two days before.

We dropped a little lower to have a good look at the procession. Since the Japs also used American-made trucks their convoys sometimes were hard to identify, but at 5,000 feet we were able to make out a red bull's-eye atop one of the trucks. That was all we needed to know.

The Japs saw us, stopped the trucks, and scattered into the ditches. We dived, each of us opening up with six .50-caliber machine guns. We could see great chunks of truck bodies, motors, and cargo flying in all directions. We had two passes at the seven machines and left three of them enveloped in flames and the others knocked to pieces.

On New Year's day, 1942, in midmorning we finished work on our airfield. By midafternoon the onrushing Japanese advance had made Lubao field front line territory. By evening we had received orders to abandon it. American infantry units, truck trains, and artillery were streaming past us on the road, bound for Bataan province where General Mac-Arthur planned to make a last stand.

The planes were divided between the 17th and 34th Pursuit Squadrons, which were sent to Pilar and Orani fields, in Bataan province, twenty and ten miles southwest of Lubao, respectively. Each squadron was alloted nine P-40s—all we had left. The remainder of the squadrons, including pilots, technicians, and ground crews, were ordered deeper into Bataan to train as a mobile infantry unit.

The two flying groups were hardly settled at their new fields, however, when they were ordered to move again. Nine planes were sent to Del Monte field, on the southern island of Mindanao, and the other nine were ordered to Bataan field, near Cabcaben, at the southeastern tip of the peninsula.

Two of the former came to grief. A lad named Wilcox was killed when his plane hit a mountainside, and another, Joseph Cole, cracked up when he ran out of gasoline. But the point is that the air defense of Bataan began with nine planes!

Those of us who trained as infantry were willing, but awkward. For nearly two weeks before we saw real action we charged up and down mountains and beat the bush for Japs. We were bivouacked in a canyon in southern Bataan and had all sorts of terrain near-by for practice.

Our equipment looked as though it might have been picked up at an ordnance rummage sale. Our weapons included some navy Marlin machine guns; air corps .50-caliber machine guns which we took from old P-40s and equipped with homemade mounts; two Browning water-cooled machine guns; six Lewis aircraft .30-caliber machine guns, which we carried over the shoulder by a leather loop, holding the barrel

38

steady with an asbestos glove, and a few Browning automatic rifles.

There were some hand grenades and four Bren gun carriers. There were only three bayonets, but this was all right

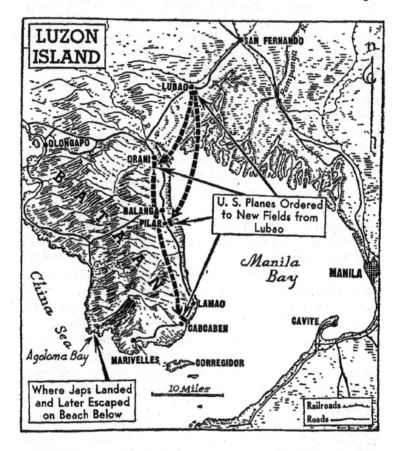

because only three of our 220 air force men knew anything about using them. We were renamed the air force battalion of the 71st division.

Our menu soon became as varied and skimpy as our armament. We had been well fixed for food on our arrival in

Bataan, but in less than two weeks the quartermaster ordered all surplus supplies turned in. From then on it was nip and tuck.

At first we had plenty of white rice. This gave way to red [unpolished] rice which was succeeded by musty red rice. There also were some cashew nuts. Hunting parties occasionally brought in deer or wild pigs.

Soon we were shooting everything edible. Before the end, there was hardly a monkey left alive in the area. We even ate lizards, though these fleet reptiles were hard to bag. In a very short time, however, we were to go after game even harder to bag.

Perhaps the bagging would have been easier if we had known a little more about the terrain and military tactics. Sometimes the mistakes we made were beyond the ludicrous.

I recall a day of maneuvers when I was acting as referee. Our men had been divided into two forces, one to hide in the jungle and the other to go in and flush them. I was walking down a jungle trail when I was amazed to hear the whistle of a bobwhite (quail). There were many things I didn't know about the Luzon jungle, but I did know there were no quail out there.

I sat down behind a clump of something and answered the whistle. There were responses from so many directions it seemed the brush must be filled with quail. I continued to whistle. Presently I could see helmeted heads poking around trees and bushes. In about ten minutes I had whistled up a full platoon.

Lieutenant James May (who was to give his life at Agoloma bay) was in command. I told him I could have cleaned out the whole bunch with a quail gun. He was as mad as a wet hen.

"I told 'em to whistle," he yelled, "but I didn't tell 'em to imitate a bunch of blankety-blank bobwhites!"

I should have been pretty stern, but Jim was in such a rage and the boys looked so aggrieved and foolish that I got to laughing and let them off with a slightly sarcastic lecture.

40

They really took their work seriously, however. We all felt we were going to be used soon. With that in prospect we held night maneuvers. We learned much, but not enough.

It was midnight of January 17 that we were awakened in our blacked out camp and hurried into waiting trucks. A seven mile ride took us to the Agoloma bay region, where the Japs had effected a landing just after dark. They now were in the jungle and, as we later learned, were preparing to advance until dawn.

Our green troops made so much noise with their yelling, shooting, and floundering, however, that the Japs thought they were facing a major force and dug in at once. We were joined by some Philippine army and constabulary units and a scattering of men from the 803d Engineers, U.S.A.

This was the start of a long siege. We had no entrenching tools and were forced to lie on top of the ground or fire from behind trees. Casualties ran high. Our food during the week to come was chiefly salmon gravy on sour-dough bread. Our water was hauled in fuel drums and reeked of gasoline.

We had been told the Jap party numbered about thirty, but the ferocity of their defense soon showed us there were hundreds of them. All night long the jungle crackled with rifle fire, punctuated by the bomblike blasts of mortar shells. There was much irregular machine gun fire—or so it seemed. We later learned the little cuties were setting off firecracker strings to simulate machine guns.

To our cost we became acquainted with their strategy of playing dead until an American column had crept past them. Then the supposed corpses would rise up and shoot the Americans in the back. We countered this by never passing a "dead" Jap without shooting him to make sure he was hors de combat. But before those seven sleepless days and nights had ended we were so weary, dirty, and starved we didn't care whether we were shot or not.

I had a hard-bitten, drawling young sergeant who was particularly adept at spotting 'possuming Japs. One day, early in the siege, I was sitting with him near the edge of a wood. He was answering my questions somewhat absently and I saw he was staring at what appeared to be a very dead Jap, lying against a tree trunk.

"Cap'n," he said at length, "I don't think that buzzard's dead."

"Well, why don't you shoot and find out?" I said.

It was the command the sergeant had hoped for. He raised his rifle and fired. The Jap bounced to a sitting position, then fell over.

The sergeant shot him twice more "to make it official." Later in the siege he caught another 'possuming Jap, but just a second too late. A general who had come down to view the action made the error of arriving with boots and ornaments polished until they gleamed. We on the firing line had long since learned to strip ourselves of all insignia because Jap snipers aim for officers.

The general came striding along, looking like something off a parade ground. Suddenly my sergeant yelled, whipped up his rifle, and fired. Another shot cracked out almost with his and the general's orderly grasped a shattered shoulder. The sergeant swore monotonously as he put three more slugs into a writhing Jap.

"I would have shot him before," the sergeant said later, "but I didn't want to startle the general. Dang it!"

Later the same day we were advancing into a particularly dense jungle sector. We knew there were Japs just ahead. Beside me was one of my squadron boys carrying a Lewis gun. It was a tense moment and, as often happens at such times, the gunner felt the need of a little levity.

"Cap'n," he said, "how will we tell which are Japs and which are monkeys?"

The sergeant answered for me.

"Just kill 'em all, son," he said. "We can eat the ones that ain't got uniforms on."

On the night the siege started we were about a quarter of a mile from the cliffs overlooking Agoloma bay. In a week we occupied 150 yards of this area on a line about 500 yards long.

Then we handed the job over to a large force of Philippine

scouts, who were well equipped with Garand rifles. We left them our automatic equipment and went back for a six-day rest, much of which we spent fighting a forest fire set by Jap incendiary bombs.

On our return we found that the scouts had occupied fifty yards more of the high jungle above the bay—at terrible cost to themselves. Their casualties had run about fifty per cent. The sight and stench of death were everywhere. The jungle, droning with insects, was almost unbearably hot.

We reinforced the scouts and shortened the line to 400 yards, penning up the Japs between us and the cliffs, which were fifty to sixty feet high. By the fifth day after our return our line was only about 300 yards and we were supported by four tanks under Lieutenant John Hay. The jungle now had been pretty well shot away, so that there was clearance for their passage.

We started our advance, directing the tanks' fire with walkie-talkies [portable radio sets]. The Japs now were crowded up to the very brink. There were hundreds of them, partially screened by the thick growth that extended to the edge. At fifty yards we could see them plainly. Beyond and below them was the blue water of the South China sea.

Suddenly, above the noise of the gunfire, we could hear shrieks and high-pitched yelling. Scores of Japs were tearing off their uniforms and leaping off the cliffs. Others were scrambling over the edge and shinnying down to fortifications prepared along the rock ledges. In a few minutes all surviving Japs had taken refuge below us and out of our sight.

We had a good view of the narrow beach, which was littered with bodies. Other Japs were running wildly up and down and plunging into the surf. We raked the beach and surf with machine gun fire, annihilating all who moved. Presently the waves were rolling in stained with blood and dotted with dead Japs.

I'll never forget the little Filipino who had set up an air-cooled machine gun at the brink and was peppering the crowded beach far below. At each burst he shrieked with laughter, beat his helmet against the ground, lay back to whoop with glee, then sat up to get in another burst.

We spent the rest of that day and the next trying to dislodge the Japs from the ledges and galleries of the cliffs. We lowered boxes of dynamite with ropes and detonated them, but with little effect. Then we tried grenades and mines, also lowered by ropes and also ineffective. It would have been suicide to have stormed them from the beach because they were well armed.

It was not until the eighth day, assisted by the navy, that we wiped them out. The navy supplied two whaleboats and two 35-foot longboats that had been plated with armor and armed with captured 37-mm. Jap cannon, twin .30-caliber machine guns and one .50-caliber gun each.

Ten men of our squadron were in each of the whaleboats. I went with one of the homemade gunboats to direct the fire. Previously we had lowered sheets over the face of the cliff to mark the Jap positions.

We stood off the beach and had shelled them for about ten minutes when a sailor hurried up to the commander (now a war prisoner) and called his attention to a flight of Jap dive bombers approaching from the east.

"To hell with the airplanes, sailor," the commander snapped. To me he said: "Where do you want the next shot, captain?"

Our little fleet raced for the beach with the Jap planes immediately above us, loosing a rain of 100-pound fragmentation bombs. They were bursting all about us, sending up geysers of water. Through it all the navy gunners continued to blast away. One of the whaleboats was hit, then one of the gunboats. In another minute the second whaleboat was gone.

Almost at the beach a near hit demolished our gunboat. There were casualties among our volunteers and the navy personnel as well. The intrepid commander was wounded critically.

But our shelling had been so deadly it was an easy matter for our survivors to storm the remaining Japs and mop them up. We finished this task at noon, taking only one prisoner.

44

He fled over the top of the cliff and into the arms of our men waiting there.

We counted more than 600 Jap bodies in the jungle, in the ledge, and on the beach. Many others were carried away by the sea. And we had been sent after only thirty!

That night in our old bivouac area we slept like the dead. There was no duty on the day following. We spent it luxuriously, bathing in the mountain stream, getting into clean clothing, and cutting one another's hair. Getting spruced up a little raised our spirits a hundred per cent.

I had finished and was climbing the slope when the path was blocked by an amazing apparition. It was my sergeant, but how changed! I grabbed for my .45 before recognizing him.

His hair had been cropped so closely his head was burred like a Jap's. Around his neck hung a pair of Jap binoculars. At his hip was a Jap automatic. Across his chest was a ponderous Jap watch chain, supporting ten watches.

All around his person other watches and Jap pendants dangled and glittered in the sun. Completing the get-up was a pair of big Jap spectacles, which he wore on his forehead as elderly ladies sometimes do.

"You'd better get rid of some of that Jap junk," I said, letting my pistol slip back into the holster. "And you'd better do it before you go down where those other guys are. You know how trigger happy everybody is today."

"That's right, cap'n," he said. "I'm going to. I know what I'll do. I know where I can trade these binoculars for a Jap saber!"

Soon afterward, General George paid us a visit and we presented him with a captured Japanese saber. With it was a note which read:

"We, the members of the 21st Pursuit Squadron, who have served as engineers, infantry, artillery, anti-parachute troops, anti-sniper troops, mechanized units, marines, and air corps— our first and only love—respectfully present as a token of our

45

esteem this Japanese saber, taken in the battle of Agoloma bay."

And it developed that General George had not merely dropped in to pass the time of day. He touched off a wild charivari of clanging tinware, shots, and Indian yells by letting it be known we soon would be back with our first love. The 21st Pursuit was assigned to Bataan and Cabcaben fields. We would be in the air again.

CHAPTER THREE

WHEN WE JOINED THE REMNANTS of several other flying organizations on Bataan and Cabcaben fields February 13, 1942, we found that our Philippines air force had grown from nine to ten planes. But that was little to rejoice about.

The original nine had been good P-40s. Of these only five remained. The other planes, some of them flown in from the southern islands, included an O-1 army biplane, a ramshackle Bellanca, a dilapidated Beechcraft, and a couple of other jobs. These boneyard ships were called the Bamboo Fleet and were kept at Bataan field along with three of the P-40s.

The other P-40s were assigned to Cabcaben field, a mile to the west. Both fields began at the water's edge and sloped upward toward the Mariveles mountains. They were at the southeastern tip of Bataan peninsula and each had a single runway. We always took off southeast, no matter how the wind set, and came in over the water to land northwest.

The planes were hidden in the jungle at the upper end of the field. General George had a shack at the edge of Bataan field to be near his men. We built our mess hall in a little canyon, digging out the mountainside. We lived in bamboo shelters and huts near-by. The area was well protected by anti-aircraft batteries.

During the rest of February, through March and up to the fall of Bataan in early April we flew reconnaissance, brought in medical supplies from the southern islands with the Bamboo Fleet, and dropped supplies to our guerrillas who were fighting in the mountains of Luzon.

In addition, we went on bombing missions. A warrant officer, now a prisoner of the Japs, built ingenious bomb releases for our planes. My P-40, which I named "Kibosh," would carry a 300- or 500-pound egg. Some of the others could take 100-pounders or six 30-pound fragmentation bombs. And speaking of bombs, the Japs let us have it every day.

Our runway constantly was under repair, but none of their bombs ever hit our planes. Meanwhile work was in progress on a new field just north of Mariveles, a small seaport eight miles west. About this time Captain Joseph Moore of Mississippi, who was in charge at Mariveles, raised an old navy duck [amphibious plane] that had been sunk in the early days of the war.

Joe got it to flying and used it to bring in supplies, medicine, and official mail. On nearly every trip he would manage to include several boxes of candy for the boys. The duck was named "The Candy Clipper."

The candy was manna. Our food situation was growing rapidly worse. We were eating lizards, monkeys, and anything else that came under our guns. We set off dynamite in the water in the hope of getting fish, but the blasts usually burst the fishes' floats and they sank. The life expectancy of anything that walked, crawled, or flew on lower Bataan was practically nil.

The food shortage was cause for uneasiness even at the start and it grew swiftly critical. At no time did we have beef. Now and then we killed a carabao [water buffalo] and boiled its dark, strong, tough meat. We had a formula for cooking carabao: you put a stone in the pot with it and when the stone melted the carabao was cooked.

Late in February we slaughtered the last horses and mules

of the 26th Cavalry, receiving two issues each of horse and mule meat. By this time bread, even the sour-dough variety, was a memory. There was no flour, coffee, sugar, powdered milk, or jelly. One of the last rations I drew included nine medium-sized cans of salmon and forty-five pounds of musty red rice—for 175 men.

The chow line hardly ever formed that someone didn't collapse from hunger and weakness. Malaria began taking its toll, also. Many of the pilots would have been incapable of flying even if we had had the planes. Only one thing was plentiful. Our source of clear cold water was a sparkling little stream fed by a high mountain spring.

Occasionally there would be a feast amid the famine. Our engineering officer, whom we called "Jitter Bill," suggested to General George that he be allowed to fly the old Bellanca of the Bamboo Fleet to Cebu.

His idea was to load it up with medicines and food in the southern islands to relieve our situation. General George was enthusiastic. Bill made two trips, returning from the first with five three-gallon tins of quinine, and a quantity of blood plasma and gas gangrene serum. In addition, he brought food which he had stacked under the seats, stuffed inside his shirt, and taped and tied all through the old plane.

These pioneering flights really brought the Bamboo Fleet into the picture and gave it a purpose in life. Other of the old crates were taken on foraging flights. Captain Whitfield began flying the Beechcraft. Captains Dick Fellows and William Cummings took two more of the rattletraps on grub missions. Their combined efforts helped, of course, but 175 to 220 hungry mouths can make an appalling amount of food disappear.

Jitter Bill came to be looked upon as the chief of the Bamboo Fleet. He was a character I'll long remember. His nickname came from no lack of nerve. No one in the squadron was braver. Day after day he flew the condemned and unarmed Bellanca, taking missions that sometimes appeared to be hopeless.

But he was jittery; there is no question about that. He

probably was the only man in the air forces who would try to wind his eight-day panel clock six times an hour. His speech was jerky and rapid-fire. You'd walk toward him to say something, but before you'd get your mouth open he would pop out with:

"You bet, boy! That's right. That's right." And Bill ended all conversations, no matter the topic, with: "Thank you, boy. Good luck, boy."

Before the war Bill had been pilot for a commercial air line in the islands. Sometimes he would forget he now was in the army. One night he was to fly three colonels to Mindanao. Bill walked over without saluting and, from force of habit, picked up one of the handbags and hefted it. The grip weighed almost a hundred pounds.

"God almighty, man!" Bill bellowed. "Whattaya got in there? Bricks? Don't you know you're only allowed thirty pounds?"

The amazed colonel took a step backward. Bill opened his mouth again, but closed it abruptly and scrambled into the plane. We explained matters to the colonel, who was a nice fellow and left most of his belongings behind. Some colonels —and there must have been a thousand of them in the Philippines—were not such nice fellows. When we began evacuating them to the southern islands we could take only three at a time and there were some terrible rows over who ranked whom. It was my job to sort them out and provide passage for the three who ranked the others. The boys used to gather outside my shack to hear the shouting:

"I rank you by thirty-two days!"

"Yes, but you don't rank ME!"

"Who says I don't?"

Most of us will remember Jitter Bill for his last mission from Bataan field. It was as fine an example of calm courage as I ever expect to see. It became necessary that someone fly a plane of the Bamboo Fleet to Corregidor on an urgent matter, then proceed to Mindanao. The rub was that it would be necessary to refuel at the field on the island of Panay. And there was no way of knowing whether or not that.

field was in our hands or the Japs'. The fellows voted to cut for low card to determine who would get the job. Bill frowned at this and told two friends he did not intend to let any young and less experienced pilot get the assignment.

After some talk Bill brought in the deck, which was shuffled and spread out. Everyone reached for a card. Bill took his and stepped far back. When the showdown came, he walked back to the table and laid down the deuce of clubs. The others were suspicious, but Bill shook a finger at them.

"You boys just ain't livin' right; ain't livin' right," he said. Then he went off to warm up his plane. The last I saw of Bill he was industriously winding his panel clock.

He completed the mission safely, but was taken prisoner at Mindanao.

On March 1. General George called me in and said he thought we ought to have a party. I asked him with whom and with what. He said with the nurses from Hospital No. 2 —a few miles away—and with whatever we could scare up.

"If this war is going to be fought by our boys and girls, Ed," he said, "they might as well have what little good times they can."

We had some extra gasoline one of our pilots had spotted in a forgotten jungle supply dump. We had brought it into camp. We mixed kerosene with it to tone it down for use in the trucks in which we drove over to pick up the nurses.

The party itself was held in a thatched shack which we used as a clubhouse. Its walls were decorated with Jap helmets, rifles, sabers, and other trophies. There was a scoreboard with the records of our pilots; number of planes downed, citations, and so on. Over the door were mounted some fine carabao antlers with a placard which read:

THE DYSENTERY CROSS
Awarded to the Quartermaster by
THE MEN OF BATAAN FIELD

We sported a battered piano we had fished from the rubble of a bombed out village, and a corporal and a buck sergeant to play it. They were talented exponents of boogie woogie. Between dances they would sit together at the piano and cut loose till the roof rocked.

Among our dozen guests were Lieutenant Juanita Redmond and Lieutenant Helen L. Summers. They wore civilian dresses and we were in our best handwashed, unironed uniforms, without ties. It had been so long since we had seen white women we were shy and awkward. This didn't wear off until almost time for them to start home.

Some of the boys had brought in crackers and cookies and a few containers of relish spread. We drank canned pineapple juice.

We danced on canvas spread over the bamboo floor. Despite our boys' hot music there was no jitterbugging. We were too tired and the shack wouldn't have taken it. Our second party was ruined by a beautiful full moon.

Its silvery light would have been conducive to romance anywhere else in the world. But on Bataan it meant only that if the Japs had effected a landing before moonrise, they would be attacking soon. So, we thought more about the Japs than about our pretty dancing partners. But we weren't called out.

The day after this the bomb release on my plane Kibosh was completed just about the time our lookout in the Mariveles mountains reported a large number of Japanese ships entering Subic bay, which begins at the northwestern corner of Bataan and gouges deeply into Zambales province to the north. I immediately asked General George if we could try our luck with a few 500-pounders.

"No, Ed," he said. "We'll proceed on the same line we've been following. The time isn't right yet."

The next morning, however, I got a message from air force headquarters to get to the field immediately. On the way I met our operations officer, Lieutenant Ben S. Brown of Hawkinsville, Ga.

"Well, Ed," he said. "We are putting the big shoes on Joe. Everything'll be ready when you get there." He was using the double talk we employed on our radio to confuse the Japs. Putting the big shoes on Joe meant loading a plane with a

500-pound bomb. Putting the little shoes on meant that six 30-pound fragmentations were going into the racks.

I went to General George's shack. He told me the Japs were unloading a vast amount of supplies near Olongapo, Zambales, in the eastern reach of Subic bay and about thirty air miles from Bataan field. In view of their numbers, General George considered it best to discourage them as much as possible. As I left he called: "Be careful, Ed." I told him I would, then hurried to the field.

Kibosh was waiting with a big green 500-pound bomb slung underneath. Lieutenant Posten, who had taken off earlier with six fragmentation bombs, returned about this time. He had dropped his load, but didn't know whether he had damaged any of the Jap ships.

I took off at 12:30 P.M., followed by Shorty, another pilot now a prisoner of war. It was his job to weave along behind me and keep Japs off my tail. I climbed to 10,000 feet over the sea, then headed north and west. When I was even with Subic bay I headed across to start my dive with the sun at my back.

When I got in close, however, I saw that the big ship concentration was not at Olongapo, as I had been told, but out near Grand island about seven miles farther on and midway of the bay's 3½-mile mouth. There were a dozen or more vessels there, busily unloading. I headed for them.

Ten thousand feet below me Subic bay lay smooth as a floor except for the feathery wakes of Japanese transports and warships.

On the inner or north side of the island two transports were unloading. Two cruisers, two destroyers and two transports were well inside the harbor while others were just outside it. A large transport was entering, passing between Grand island and the western shore. I chose this as my target.

It was a beautiful, cloudless flying day. The scene below me was like a brilliant lithograph, the colors almost too real. At 5,000 feet, with the throttle wide open, I saw that I was to receive a big-time reception. Anti-aircraft batteries opened up from the island and most of the ships.

At 2,000 feet I released my 500-pound bomb and began to pull out of the dive. Looking back, I saw it miss the big transport by 40 feet and send a great geyser of white water skyward. I was pretty hot at the miss, so I pulled around and gave the Jap the .50-caliber treatment.

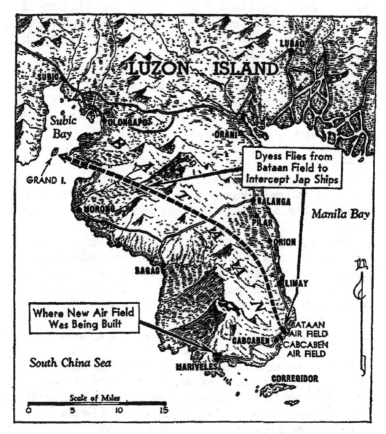

I strafed him three times, from stern to bow, bow to stern —concentrating on the bridge—and from stern to bow again. How much damage, if any, my bomb accomplished I don't know.

During the strafing, however, the transport stopped dead

and didn't move again that day. The anti-aircraft fire was coming up in earnest now, so I pulled around the island and blistered four small warehouses on the shore near the two freighters which were unloading. From there I could see two 100-ton motor vessels plying between the island and the Bataan shore.

I caught one of them well out in the open and concentrated on its two forward guns, then started firing amidships into the hull, hoping to get the engine room. By this time I was just above the water and coming in fast.

The Japs aboard her were putting on quite an act. Those astern were running forward and those forward were rushing astern. They couldn't have done better for my purpose. They met amidships where my bullets were striking. When I was 100 yards from the ship I veered off to north, banked around, and went in again the same way.

The concentrated fire of six .50-caliber guns literally was knocking the sides out of her. Suddenly she stopped, listed, and began to sink. I got in one short burst at her sister ship, then ran out of ammunition. I couldn't see Shorty but I called to him on the radio, telling him we were all washed up.

When I returned to Bataan field I found two large holes and a small one in my wings. Shorty landed at Cabcaben field, untouched. When I landed, Captain Joe Moore sent two pilots from Mariveles field, eight miles west of us, in P-40s to drop fragmentation bombs. One of these kids, Lieutenant White, dropped his on the dock area at Olongapo.

When White came out of his dive, however, the other youngster had disappeared. We finally concluded that because of his inexperience he had followed the leading plane too closely and had been caught by anti-aircraft fire. This had happened many times before, and most seasoned pilots were wise to the hazard.

While Kibosh was being refueled and loaded with another 500-pounder and ammunition, I sent Lieutenant Sam Grashio to drop a load of frags on Grand island. His homemade bomb release jammed, however, and he was forced to land on Mariveles field still fully loaded. This was a touchy undertaking, but there was nothing else to do except bail out. And Sam knew we could not afford to lose the plane.

When Kibosh was ready, I took off and made the same approach to Subic bay. The situation was practically unchanged. I picked the two unloading freighters as my target and went into a dive at 10,000 feet, again releasing the bomb at 2,000. It passed just over the outer freighter and exploded among a concentration of barges and lighters that were receiving cargo from the ships. They went up in a glorious cloud of smoke, water, and debris. I felt better.

As I pulled up, swarms of Japs began running from the two ships and stampeding along the dock toward shore. I pulled around and cleaned off the dock with my machine guns. While in the vicinity I sprayed the four warehouses again with everything I had. Then I went for the second of the two 100-ton motor vessels. I gave it a long burst and it caught fire from end to end. It soon sank.

There was a long tanker near-by which received the last of my ammunition, apparently with no ill-effects. I gave Shorty the high sign, and we went home.

I was glad to get back. I should mention that I was fighting on two fronts that day—both against the Japs and against diarrhea.

The boys swarmed around Kibosh. They found several more A-A holes while they were servicing it and slinging a new 500-pound bomb into the rack. General George was reluctant when I indicated I was planning a third visit to the bay. He eventually granted permission. If he hadn't, I'd have missed the best shooting of the day.

Lieutenant John Burns—later killed in Mindanao—went along as my tail weaver this time. After making the same old approach to Subic, I went into a dive at 10,000 feet just at sundown. I soon saw that my two freighters had shoved out from the dock and were running around like mad.

I therefore aimed my bomb at the enormous supply dumps which had been built up along the northern shore of Grand island, around the warehouses and beyond. I held to the dive until I was at about 1,800 feet, then turned loose the bomb. It was a direct hit.

There was a terrific explosion that scattered flaming debris all over the island. A fierce fire started almost immediately near the middle of the island. It burned all night and part of the next day.

It was deep twilight now, which made it hard to see the ships. But I had no difficulty in seeing the A-A fire which was streaming up from all directions. Cruisers, destroyers, and shore batteries had all cut loose. They really were filling the sky. I told General George later that with his permission I would do my future strafing in daylight. At night those tracers look too big and too many.

Meanwhile our observers on Mariveles mountain reported to air force headquarters that a large transport was slipping out of the bay. When this was relayed to me I flew north across the bay until the ship was silhouetted against the glow in the west. I started the attack by strafing it from amidships to the stern. Small fires leaped up all over the after deck.

There was no trouble in hitting that baby. It was plenty big. I could see plainly my six streams of .50-caliber tracers and could put them just where I wanted. I climbed to 4,000 feet, then came back, laying my fire along the bow and putting it into the bridge. Fires started all over the bow and in the well deck. Then she blew up. My plane was at 1,800 feet and diving at 45 degrees.

There was a blinding flash from below. A black cloud of debris-filled smoke shot into the sky, far above me. I yanked back on the stick to avoid flying into the shower of wreckage. The ship responded so suddenly I blacked out colder than a pair of ice tongs. I was out several seconds and when I came to, the P-40 was hanging by its propeller at about 4,000 feet.

The water below was a mass of flame. A few minutes later there was nothing where the ship had been.

The glow in the west now served me well a second time. Silhouetted against it was a fairly large ship that had been reported variously as a cruiser, destroyer, tanker, and transport. It was so dark I couldn't tell what it was, but it sent up more A-A than any tanker or transport I ever have tackled.

When I started my dive the ship was turning rapidly, as though trying to get back into the bay. I struck from the southwest, raking it from bow to stern.

The ship stopped turning and put on speed, heading

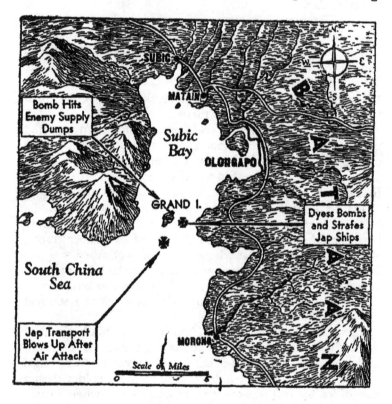

straight out into the South China sea. I hit at the Jap next from the northeast, strafing him from stern to bow. As I slid over him all anti-aircraft guns had been silenced and small fires were blazing up on both the bow and stern. When I came around to hit him again from the southwest, the fires had grown much larger.

I gave him another raking from bow to stern, with special

attention to the bridge. It was the most thorough treatment of the three and during it I expended the last of my ammunition. I was trying to make it blow up as the other ship had, but without success. It ended up as a total loss, however. It burned all night after being beached and still was burning the next day.

It was so dark now I couldn't see Burns's plane, but I gave him the high sign and started home. The glow from below showed me a number of large bullet holes in my P-40. And now, I did the stupidest thing of my flying career.

Instead of flying low over the water to get safely within our lines, I blandly cut across the shore line at about 1,000 feet—directly over Jap territory. I was booming along, thinking of nothing in particular when up came such a cloud of anti-aircraft fire as I never have seen before or since. Tracers were sailing at me from every direction at once.

I nearly jumped out of my skin. I never have been so mad at myself or anyone else. I turned away, climbing and weaving—and holding my breath. The sky was so full of fire it was like flying down Broadway. The P-40 was catching hell. This, I figured, probably was the finish and I deserved it. Somehow or other, with fool's luck, I made it unscratched.

Nearing the field, I realized I had a terrific tail wind. I went in over the water and set the P-40 down to a pretty bum landing, but I didn't care much. The boys rushed up and as I jumped out I told them:

"We got one that time."

[When Colonel Dyess landed on that night of March 3, 1942, his score for the day was one 12,000-ton transport blown up and sunk, one 5,000- or 6,000-ton vessel burned, two 100-ton motor vessels sunk, a number of barges and lighters destroyed, a vast amount of supplies and material blown up and burned, plus a large but undetermined number of Japanese killed in the sinkings and repeated strafings of Grand island and its docks. The Tokio radio announced the next day that Subic bay had been raided by three flights of four-engined bombers, escorted by fighter planes.]

Just as I hit the ground I saw a stream of tracers going up

against the mountain from beyond the hill that separated Bataan field and Cabcaben. I thought at first we had drawn some "flies"—Jap bombers—as it was their habit to bomb hell out of us right after each of our raids. Then I realized the direction of the fire meant it was coming from Burns's plane. I supposed he had pressed the firing button accidentally after landing.

At General George's headquarters I got the bad news. The tail wind had brought Burns in too fast and to avoid over-shooting the field, he had groundlooped the P-40, damaging it severely, but escaping serious injury himself. It was during the loop that his guns had fired.

With General George were Captain (now Lieutenant Colonel) Allison W. Ind of Ann Arbor, Mich., his aide; Lieutenant Ben Brown, and Major (now Lieutenant Colonel) Lefty Eades. I had just finished telling them my story when the really bad news came in. Two pilots who had been sent up from Mariveles field to cover the landing of Burns and myself had both cracked up in the tail wind. The planes were beyond repair.

We had lost one of our five P-40's in Subic bay in the afternoon, Burns had cracked up another in the same tail wind that undid the Mariveles boys; thus the latest disasters left us with only mine. In addition there were only the Candy Clipper and the Bamboo Fleet. The Mariveles boys were young and had done very little flying in the last few weeks. General George rallied first.

"Forget it," he said. "We couldn't have done better and this was bound to happen sooner or later." Then, from the depths of his luggage, he came up with a quart of whisky. We were bowled over, but no one said anything except "Here's how!" Though General George spoke lightly of the aircraft loss, he felt deeply the death of the pilot. Losing one of his boys always was a personal sorrow.

Pretty soon someone remembered that a prank note written a few days before by a newspaper correspondent had been ominously prophetic. The note, addressed to President

Roosevelt, had read: "Dear Mr. President: Please send us another P-40. The one we have is all shot up."

When the crew finished with old Kibosh the next day it looked like a patchwork quilt. The plane was olive drab and the external patches were bright blue. There were sixty-five or seventy of them. You could hardly see Kibosh for the patches.

The next morning General George dug again into his reserves and came up with flour, baking powder, and coffee. He made hotcakes for Ind, Eades, and me.

After breakfast I got to thinking about our situation. I felt pretty somber. Our losses of the night before had been serious. The Jap loss had been far greater, but they could replace their men and matériel. We couldn't. We were outnumbered in aircraft, men, ordnance—in everything. We had to strike when and where we could. I thought, rather prophetically, that ours were guerrilla tactics and should be expanded along that field.

We even had to improvise much equipment. Among other things, we invented belly tanks which we welded from sheet metal and which served also as incendiary bombs. They were finned and equipped with shotgun shells and firing pins to set them off when they hit. There was an ingenious arrangement which permitted us to run the plane on the gasoline they contained, when necessary. These now were in what we called mass production—about two a week.

On March 5 Leo, the lieutenant who was my new engineering officer, assisted by men of the 21st Pursuit Squadron, finished construction of an additional plane. In it were parts from all the P-40s and P-40Es that had been cracked up. We called it the P-40-Something. It flew quite well. Shortly afterward we were reinforced by two well-worn P-35s from Mindanao.

We put bomb racks on them and on the P-40-Something. Thus we had four fighting ships in addition to the Candy Clipper and the Bamboo Fleet. These planes were our air force at the fall of Bataan, which now was only about three weeks away.

CHAPTER FOUR

On an afternoon in mid-March, 1942, I set my P-40 down on Bataan field after a reconnaissance flight and found General George waiting for me.

"I guess this is good-by for a while, Ed," he said. Then he told me he had been ordered to accompany General MacArthur, who was going to Australia to take supreme command of our forces in the Southwest Pacific. It was obvious to me that General George was leaving us only with the greatest reluctance.

"Tell the boys," he said, "that if I'm not back pretty soon it will not be because I don't want to come back."

It was the last time I ever saw him. He was one of the grandest officers I ever have known. We always thought of him as a genius who was human. [General George lost his life in an airplane accident in Australia a few weeks later.]

At the time he left us our food shortage had grown acute. More than sixty per cent of our pilots were so weakened by hunger they were incapable of flying the planes. Those who did fly came back from missions completely used up.

At some meals we had only rice. At others there was only a thin salmon soup. Salmon gravy had been unheard of since our flour supply had given out. Occasionally there was a bird or two or a monkey. At length, our flight surgeon, Lieutenant Colonel William Keppard, determined something had to be done.

He put it up to Major General Edward P. King, straight from the shoulder. In a very short time there would be no more flying unless the pilots were given proper food. General King arranged at once for extra rations to be sent over from Corregidor. There were to be full rations and vitamin tablets for twenty-five fliers for ten days. As soon as this was assured I called in several of our sergeants.

I told them there was to be extra food for some of the

pilots, but that I didn't want to issue it until I had learned the attitude of the enlisted men. The first sergeant, R. W. Houston, spoke up with feeling.

"Hell, captain," he said, "we already know all about it. The men think it's wonderful you're going to get extra grub. They said that if the new stuff isn't enough they'll give you theirs!"

I've never felt prouder to be an American.

In a day or two we were having ham, bread, peas, pineapple juice, canned corned beef hash, sugar, coffee, vitamin tablets and other items. We had hoped for cigarettes, too. In those days you were out of luck for smokes unless you had a friend on Corregidor.

The food worked a miracle almost overnight. Because of it, those favored pilots did much better than the other men during the Death March from Bataan, which was just ahead. The last red days before the surrender now were upon us, and they were an unending hell.

Jap planes were overhead constantly, bombing and strafing. Our artillery had been pushed back so far it had to send its shells whistling over our airfield to reach the enemy. Communications were practically nonexistent. Bombs and shells severed our lines as fast as they were repaired.

The wounded were pouring back night and day along the road that bisected Bataan and Cabcaben airfields. Those men not wounded were sleepless, exhausted, and bedraggled. Some of them, in their bewilderment, had become separated from their units. There were few outfits left intact, and the Japs daily were throwing in fresh troops.

Our planes were grounded on April 7 and 8, the last two days before the tragic 9th of April when Bataan was surrendered. On each of the last few nights Jap warships pulled in close and shelled us with everything they had. On the 8th their shells found our bivouac area and made a shambles of it.

In addition white phosphorus bombs were dropped, touching off the brush, so we had to do duty as fire fighters. None of us got any sleep. We were all crazy to go after the Japs

62

with the P-40, the P-40-Something and the P-35s. But we were being saved for use in the event the enemy should try a landing behind our lines.

There was a nebulous project afoot concerning supply ships from Cebu island. We were to "shoot down all Japanese aircraft" that tried to interfere and were to be assisted by bombers supposedly en route from Australia. PT boats were to attack and harass blockading Jap surface ships. But all this had been set for April 10, and it never materialized.

I left the field an hour before sundown on the 8th, returning to the bivouac area to check the damage. I needed sleep, too.

We were expecting a plane of the Bamboo Fleet with medical supplies from Cebu and I planned to help unload it. I had just sat down to eat when there was an emergency call from the field. Captain Burt of Alabama—now a prisoner of war—told me a powerful Jap force had broken through our lines and was only two miles down the road from the field.

I jumped into a car and started. The road was choked with Filipino troops in wild retreat. It was sundown when I got to the landing strip. There I grabbed Lieutenant Jack Donaldson, Tulsa, Okla., and told him to take off in old Kibosh with six 30-pound fragmentation bombs and to bomb and strafe the approaching Japs.

Jack had been with me in the infantry days. He was what we called an "eager beaver"—always ready for a scrap. I said:

"Jack, after you have finished, come back to the field. If this is a false alarm, come in and land. If the Japs are as close as they tell us, rock your wings and keep going—for Cebu."

He was back in fifteen minutes with his bomb racks empty. He rocked the plane like all hell and kept going. I later learned he made Cebu all right, but that one of the ship's hydraulic lines had been shot out so that he had to land with the wheels up. That was the end of faithful old Kibosh.

By this time I had got through to air force headquarters and told them the situation. They told me at once to start evacuating the pilots in our remaining planes. They specified the pilots who were to go. Shortly afterward Captain Joe

Moore took off from Cabcaben field in a P-40 and Captain O. L. Lunde took off from Bataan in a P-35. He took an extra pilot, doubled up in the baggage compartment.

At dark the artillery back of the field opened up on the Japs down the road. Simultaneously our forces started blowing up the ammunition dumps a quarter of a mile from the field.

I got all the planes out on the field with their motors running in the event the Japs should break through unexpectedly. Then I called headquarters and told Captain Hank Thorne and Ben Brown to come to the field. I met them on a rise near-by and ordered them into the remaining P-35 which was waiting. They both refused to go, but as the field commanding officer I sent them off.

These two had done wonderful work on Bataan. Hank had headed the 3rd Pursuit Squadron which fought at Eba the first day of the war. Ben Brown was one of the foremost air heroes of Bataan, downing many Jap planes and bombing and strafing landing parties with deadly effect.

Hank and Ben took another pilot with them in their battered P-35, which they got into the air by the light of the exploding ammunition dumps. Hank also took six fragmentation bombs which he dropped on the advancing Japs.

Our ground crews, meanwhile, were working like beavers, emptying and lighting gasoline stores, smashing radios, and pulling out our guns at the edge of the field. We left the place as clean as a whistle. The Japs got nothing. Air force ordnance men soon arrived and began blowing up our bombs.

I assembled the available pilots and men and we took all the guns we could get transportation for. We destroyed the rest. We then hurried to Cabcaben field and found that all planes except the Candy Clipper had gone. On its last flight it had blown a cylinder.

Leo had worked on it twenty-four hours without a letup, installing a cylinder he had taken from the wreck of another navy plane. He had the motor running, but as the

Clipper had not been test hopped, no one knew whether it would fly.

I loaded it up with Lieutenants Barnek, Robb, Coleman, Shorty, and Boelens. At the last minute I put in Colonel Carlos Romulo, who had been sent over by Lieutenant General Jonathan Wainwright from Corregidor that night. Romulo had been a newspaper man and after entering military service was attached to General MacArthur's headquarters.

[*Dyess had been ordered to leave in the first plane for the south. Others, whom he evacuated, stated afterward he had refused to leave the men who could not be taken. Of this, Dyess said only that "different arrangements were made, with permission, of course."*]

The old Candy Clipper did herself proud. Though heavily loaded, she got off beautifully. Barnek was the pilot. He had been on duty at headquarters throughout his stay on Bataan. As the Clipper lifted from the strip, Corregidor's artillery opened up in support of the Bataan batteries. Shells were bursting just down the road. The racket was terrific.

I took the men remaining on the field and, with our guns and such food as could be rustled up, we started for Mariveles, where we were to reorganize as mobile infantry. Just before we reached Little Baguio, about four miles west of Cabcaben, hell really broke loose. They were blowing up the main munitions dumps, the engineers' dynamite dumps, and others. The navy was setting off its dumps and destroying its tunnels near Mariveles.

Almost anywhere on lower Bataan you could have read a newspaper by the lurid glare. Artillery still was pounding away and shell fragments were screaming through the air. Because some of the exploding dumps were near the road, it was impossible to advance for some time.

It was daylight when we reached Mariveles. I left some of the pilots on the Mariveles cutoff. The men with the guns and food went to a point two and one-half miles north of the town to wait. I had been ordered to keep them readily accessible in the event we should find transportation off the peninsula.

Late in the morning we were told General King had surrendered Bataan's defenders to the Imperial Japanese army. As the official word spread, one of the most disheartening scenes of my life unfolded just outside the town. Our army

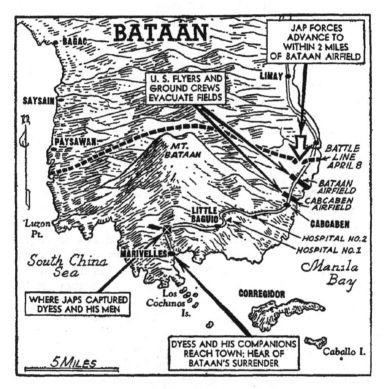

trucks, rumbling down the dust fogged roads all hoisted white flags. Individuals held up pieces of white cloth as they walked along.

The Japs continued to bomb and shell the area without letup. Filipino men, women, and children were huddled in dazed groups along the road or were running wildly about. Their outcries mingled with the rumble of trucks and the shriek and thud of heavy shellfire in a symphony of despair.

American and Filipino wounded lay unattended in the dust. Other American soldiers, wounded days before, were wandering through the pall still in hospital pajamas and kimonos. They had been left homeless by the bombing of Hospital No. 1.

I took one group of pilots through the ruined streets of Mariveles to the waterfront in the hope of getting a boat in which they could make a run for Corregidor, three miles distant by water.

On the way, I saw a little Philippine scout who had been my runner during the action of Agoloma bay. He was a powerfully built youngster and a real fighter. We called him "El Toro"—The Bull. I asked him what he was doing. He pointed to a critically wounded man lying near-by.

"Sir," he said, "I stay with my wounded companion." When we passed back that way Toro was still there, but his companion had died.

There was no transportation for my pilots. The boats that escaped destruction during the bombing already had been taken.

I knew where our guerrillas could be found, but they were a long way off. We had got ample food from the navy when we passed their exploding tunnels, but we had no quinine. I hesitated to take to the malaria-ridden hills without it. A number of men, not of our squadron, tried it and they were pitiable sights when they were caught. Some may have made it; others certainly perished on the way.

So our party headed northward out of town to rejoin the ground crews with the guns and the food. We had covered about two miles and were ascending a steep, ledgelike road, when we came face to face with three Jap tanks, standing side by side and blocking our path. Standing out of an open turret was a Jap officer I'll never forget. Of his face I could see nothing but squinting eyes and buck teeth. He was pointing an automatic pistol at us.

We stopped. We were prisoners. The Jap waved his gun, motioning us down off the road into a depression beside it.

The Japs had all the hills and elevations. Tanks were charging up and down, firing their machine guns into treetops. Lines of marching Japs were silhouetted against the sky along all the high places. Planes still were bombing the area. Shells continued to fall. The jig certainly was up, for the time being anyway.

None of us had had any rest for four days and nights. We decided, therefore, to eat something, get a little sleep, and plan our next move.

But no countermove ever was planned or executed. After eating we sank into dreamless sleep and knew nothing until the Jap guards awakened us early the next morning. Marching in a pall of dust stirred up by the wheels of Jap trucks, we were herded to the landing strip north of Mariveles. There our guards arranged us in long lines.

There still was plenty of fight left in us. We were prisoners, but we didn't feel licked. I don't know what we would have felt could we have known that this was only the first of 361 days to be filled with murder and cruelty such as few American soldiers ever have endured. It was the start of the Death March from Bataan.

CHAPTER FIVE

NORTH OF THE NARROW flying field stood Mount Bataan, its jagged crater rising 4,600 feet above us into the clear, cool sky. From these upper reaches came the drone of Jap dive bombers, circling endlessly. To the south, smoke still was rising from the rubble which a few days before had been Mariveles.

Three miles away, across the harbor's blue-green waters

the rocky eminence of Corregidor stood unconquered, still guarding the sea approaches to a Manila that had fallen. Grayish smoke puffs blossomed along the sides and pinnacles of the Rock as high-flying Jap bombers dropped their loads.

The dust that enveloped Mariveles field was being stirred up by the wheels of trucks and gun carriages. Jap artillery was preparing to open fire on Corregidor from the sunken rice paddies and near-by ridges. From the pall of smoke and dust new prisoners—American and Filipino soldiers—emerged in lines and groups to join those of us already there, awaiting the pleasure of the Imperial Japanese army.

The first thing I heard after our arrival was an urgent whispering which came to us from all sides. "Get rid of your Jap stuff, quick!"

"What Jap stuff?" we whispered back.

"Everything; money, souvenirs. Get rid of it!" We did so without delay—and just in time. Jap noncommissioned officers and three-star privates were moving among us ordering that packs be opened and spread out. They searched our persons, then went through the other stuff, confiscating personal articles now and then.

I noticed that the Japs, who up to now had treated us with an air of cool suspicion, were beginning to get rough. I saw men shoved, cuffed, and boxed. This angered and mystified us. It was uncalled for. We were not resisting. A few ranks away a Jap jumped up from a pack he had been inspecting. In his hand was a small shaving mirror.

"Nippon?" he asked the owner. The glass was stamped: "Made in Japan." The soldier nodded. The Jap stepped back, then lunged, driving his rifle butt into the American's face. "Yaah!" he yelled, and lunged again. The Yank went down. The raging Jap stood over him, driving crushing blows to the face until the prisoner lay insensible.

A little way off a Jap was smashing his fists into the face of another American soldier who went to his knees and received a thudding kick in the groin, He, too, it seemed, had been caught with some Japanese trifle.

We were shocked. This treatment of war prisoners was beyond our understanding. I still didn't get it, even after some one explained to me that the Japs assumed the contraband articles had been taken from the bodies of their dead. I was totally unprepared for the appalling deed that came next.

I was too far off to witness it personally, but I saw the victim afterward. We had known him. A comrade who had stood close by told me later in shocking detail what had taken place.

The victim, an air force captain, was being searched by a three-star private. Standing by was a Jap commissioned officer, hand on sword hilt. These men were nothing like the toothy, bespectacled runts whose photographs are familiar to most newspaper readers. They were cruel of face, stalwart, and tall.

"This officer looked like a giant beside the Jap private," said my informant, who must be nameless because he still is a prisoner of war. "The big man's face was as black as mahogany. He didn't seem to be paying much attention. There was no expression in his eyes, only a sort of unseeing glare.

"The private, a little squirt, was going through the captain's pockets. All at once he stopped and sucked in his breath with a hissing sound. He had found some Jap yen.

"He held these out, ducking his head and sucking in his breath to attract notice. The big Jap looked at the money. Without a word he grabbed the captain by the shoulder and shoved him down to his knees. He pulled the sword out of the scabbard and raised it high over his head, holding it with both hands. The private skipped to one side.

"Before we could grasp what was happening, the black-faced giant had swung his sword. I remember how the sun flashed on it. There was a swish and a kind of chopping thud, like a cleaver going through beef.

"The captain's head seemed to jump off his shoulders. It hit the ground in front of him and went rolling crazily from side to side between the lines of prisoners.

"The body fell forward. I have seen wounds, but never such a gush of blood as this. The heart continued to pump for a few seconds and at each beat there was another great spurt of blood. The white dust around our feet was turned into crimson mud. I saw that the hands were opening and closing spasmodically. Then I looked away.

"When I looked again the big Jap had put up his sword and was strolling off. The runt who had found the yen was putting them into his pocket. He helped himself to the captain's possessions."

This was the first murder. In the year to come there would be enough killing of American and Filipino soldier prisoners to rear a mountain of dead.

Our Jap guards now threw off all restraint. They beat and slugged prisoners, robbing them of watches, fountain pens, money, and toilet articles. Now, as never before, I wanted to kill Japs for the pleasure of it.

The thing that almost drove me crazy was the certainty that the officer who had just been murdered couldn't have taken those yen from a dead Jap. He had been in charge of an observation post far behind the lines. I doubt that he ever had seen a dead Jap.

Gradually I got control of myself. By going berserk now I would only lose my own life without hope of ever helping to even the score.

The score just now was far from being in our favor. The 160 officers and men who remained of the 21st Pursuit Squadron were assembled with about 500 other American and Filipino soldiers of all grades and ranks. They were dirty, ragged, unshaven, and exhausted. Many were half starved.

Swirling chalky dust had whitened sweat-soaked beards, adding grotesquerie to the scene. It would not have been hard to believe these were tottering veterans of 1898, returned to the battlegrounds of their youth.

We stood for more than an hour in the scalding heat while the search, with its beating and sluggings, was completed. Then the Jap guards began pulling some of the huskiest of our number out of line. These were assembled into labor gangs, to remain in the area.

I doubt that many of them survived the hail of steel Corregidor's guns later laid down on the beaches and foothills

71

of Bataan. These were men who for months had faced American iron, thrown at them by Jap guns.

Now, it appeared, they were to die under American iron thrown into their midst by American guns. As the remainder of us were marched off the field our places were taken by other hundreds of prisoners who were to follow us on the Death March from Bataan.

We turned eastward on the national highway, which crosses

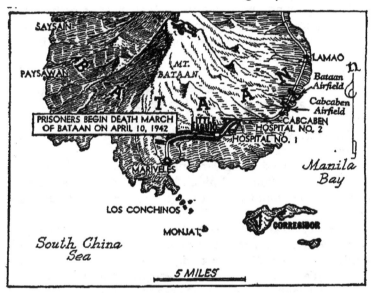

the southern tip of Bataan to Cabcaben and Bataan airfield, then veers northward through Lamao, Balanga, and Orani. From there it runs northeastward to San Fernando, the rail junction and banking town in Pampanga province.

Ordinarily, the trip from Mariveles to Cabcaben field is a beautiful one with the grandeur of high greenclad mountains on the north and a view of the sea on the right. The white of the road contrasts pleasantly with the deep green of the tropical growth on either side.

But on this day there was no beauty. Coming toward us were seemingly interminable columns of Jap infantry, truck trains, and horse-drawn artillery, all moving into Bataan for a concentrated assault on Corregidor. They stirred up clouds of blinding dust in which all shape and form were lost.

Every few yards Jap noncoms materialized like gargoyles from the grayish white pall and snatched Americans out of line to be searched and beaten. Before we had gone two miles we had been stripped of practically all our personal possessions.

The Japs made no move to feed us. Few of us had had anything to eat since the morning of April 9. Many had tasted no food in four days. We had a little tepid water in our canteens, but nothing else.

The ditches on either side of the road were filled with overturned and wrecked American army trucks, fire-gutted tanks, and artillery our forces had rendered unusable. At intervals we saw mounds of captured food, bearing familiar trademarks. These had fallen almost undamaged into Jap hands. ·

As we marched along I rounded up the 110 officers and men of the 21st Pursuit. I didn't know yet what the score was, but I felt we would be in a better position to help one another and keep up morale if we were together.

We hadn't walked far when the rumor factory opened up. In a few minutes it was in mass production. There were all kinds of reports: We were going to Manila and Old Bilibid prison. We were going to San Fernando and entrain for a distant concentration camp. Trucks were waiting just ahead to pick us up. We doubted the last rumor, but hoped it was true.

The sun was nearing the zenith now. The penetrating heat seemed to search out and dissipate the small stores of strength remaining within us. The road, which until this moment had been fairly level, rose sharply in a zigzag grade. We were nearing Little Baguio.

I was marching with head down and eyes squinted for the dual purpose of protecting myself as much as possible from the dust and glare and keeping watch on the Jap guards who walked beside and among us. Halfway up the hill we reached

73

a level stretch where a Japanese senior officer and his staff were seated at a camp table upon which were spread maps and dispatches.

As I came abreast he saw me and shouted something that sounded like, "Yoy!" He extended his hand, palm downward, and opened and closed the fingers rapidly. This meant I was to approach him. I pretended I didn't see him. He shouted again as I kept on walking. His third "Yoy!" vibrated with anger. The next I knew a soldier snatched me out of line and shoved me toward the table.

"Name!" shouted the officer. He was staring at the wings on my uniform. "You fly?"

I told him my name without mentioning my rank and said I had been a pilot.

"Where you planes?"

"All shot down." I made a downward, spinning motion with my hand.

"No at Cebu? No at Mindanao?"

"No Cebu. No Mindanao."

"Yaah. Lie! We know you got planes. We see. Sometimes one ... two ... sometimes three, four, five. Where you airfields?"

I shook my head again and made the spinning motion with my hand. But I located the airfields for him on his map. I pointed to Cabcaben, Bataan, and Mariveles. He knew about these, of course. He made an impatient gesture.

"One more. Secret field!"

"Nope. No secret field."

"True?"

"Yes. True."

"Where are tunnel? Where are underwater tunnel from Mariveles to Corregidor? Where are tunnels on Corregidor Rock?" He held the map toward me.

"I don't know of any tunnels. No tunnels; no place. I never was on Corregidor. I was only at Nichols field and Bataan."

"You flying officer and you never at Corregidor Rock!" His eyes were slits. His staff officers were angry, too. "LIE!" he shrieked and jumped up.

74

He was powerfully built, as are most Jap officers. He seized my shoulder and whirled me around with a quick twist that almost dislocated my arm. Then came a violent shove that sent me staggering toward the line. I expected a bullet to follow the push, but I didn't dare look back. This would have been inviting them to shoot. As I reached the marching line, the officer shouted something else. The guards shoved me and motioned that I should catch up with my group.

I wanted to be with them, but the double quick up the hill in the scalding heat and dust almost finished me. I had the thought, too, that the guards I passed might get the idea I was trying to escape. My bullet expectancy was so high it made my backside tingle from scalp to heels. I caught up as we were passing through Little Baguio. In a short time we were abreast the blackened ruins of Hospital No. 1, which had been bombed heavily a couple of days before.

Among the charred debris, sick and wounded American soldiers were walking dazedly about. There was no place for them to go.

Their only clothes were hospital pajama suits and kimonos. Here and there a man was stumping about on one leg and a crutch. Some had lost one or both arms. All were in need of fresh dressings. And all obviously were suffering from the shock of the bombing.

They looked wonderingly at the column of prisoners. When the Jap officers saw them, these shattered Americans were rounded up and shoved into the marching line. All of them tried to walk, but only a few were able to keep it up. Those who fell were kicked aside by the Japs.

The Japs forbade us to help these men. Those who tried it were kicked, slugged, or jabbed with bayonet points by the guards who stalked with us in twos and threes.

For more than a mile these bomb-shocked cripples stumbled along with us. Their shoulders were bent and the sweat streamed from their faces. I can never forget the hopelessness in their eyes.

Eventually their strength ebbed and they began falling

75

back through the marching ranks. I don't know what became of them.

About a mile east of the hospital we encountered a major traffic jam. On either side of the congested road hundreds of Jap soldiers were unloading ammunition and equipment.

Our contingent of more than 600 American and Filipino prisoners filtered through, giving the Japs as wide a berth as the limited space permitted. This was to avoid being searched, slugged, or pressed into duty as cargadores [burden carriers].

Through the swirling dust we could see a long line of trucks, standing bumper to bumper. There were hundreds of them. And every last one was an American make. I saw Fords —which predominated—Chevrolets, GMCs, and others.

These were not captured trucks. They bore Jap army insignia and had been landed from the ships of the invasion fleet. It is hard to describe what we felt at seeing these familiar American machines, filled with jeering, snarling Japs. It was a sort of super-sinking feeling. We had become accustomed to having American iron thrown at us by the Japs, but this was a little too much.

Eventually the road became so crowded we were marched into a clearing. Here, for two hours, we had our first taste of the oriental sun treatment, which drains the stamina and weakens the spirit.

The Japs seated us on the scorching ground, exposed to the full glare of the sun. Many of the Americans and Filipinos had no covering to protect their heads. I was beside a small bush, but it cast no shade because the sun was almost directly above us. Many of the men around me were ill.

When I thought I could stand the penetrating heat no longer, I was determined to have a sip of the tepid water in my canteen. I had no more than unscrewed the top when the aluminum flask was snatched from my hands. The Jap who had crept up behind me poured the water into a horse's nosebag, then threw down the canteen. He walked on among the prisoners, taking away their water and pouring it into the bag. When he had enough he gave it to his horse.

Whether by accident or design we had been put just

across the road from a pile of canned and boxed food. We were famished, but it seemed worse than useless to ask the Japs for anything. An elderly American colonel did, however. He crossed the road and after pointing to the food and to the drooping prisoners, he went through the motions of eating.

A squat Jap officer grinned at him and picked up a can of salmon. Then he smashed it against the colonel's head, opening the American's cheek from eye to jawbone. The officer staggered and turned back toward us, wiping the blood off.

It seemed as though the Japs had been waiting for just such a brutal display to end the scene. They ordered us to our feet and herded us back into the road.

We knew now the Japs would respect neither age nor rank. Their ferocity grew as we marched on into the afternoon. They no longer were content with mauling stragglers or pricking them with bayonet points. The thrusts were intended to kill.

We had marched about a mile after the sun treatment when I stumbled over a man writhing in the hot dust of the road. He was a Filipino soldier who had been bayoneted through the stomach. Within a quarter of a mile I walked past another. This soldier prisoner had been rolled into the path of the trucks and crushed beneath the heavy wheels.

The huddled and smashed figures beside the road eventually became commonplace to us. The human mind has an amazing faculty of adjusting itself to shock. In this case it may have been that heat and misery had numbed our senses. We remained keenly aware, however, that these murders might well be precursors of our own, if we should falter or lag.

As we straggled past Hospital No. 2 the Japs were setting up artillery and training it on Corregidor. The thick jungle hid the hospital itself, but we could see that guns were all around it. The Japs regarded this as master strategy; the Rock would not dare return their fire. I wondered what the concussion of the heavy guns would do to the stricken men in the hospital wards. The cannonade began after we had passed by.

A few minutes later a violent blow on the head almost sent me to my knees. I thought one of the Jap guns had made a direct hit on me. My steel helmet jammed down over my eyes with a clang that made my ears ring. I pulled it clear and staggered around to see a noncommissioned Jap brandishing a club the size of a child's baseball bat. He was squealing and pointing to the dented helmet. He lifted the club again. I threw the helmet into the ditch and he motioned me to march on. Like many of my comrades, I now was without protection against the merciless sun.

Jap artillery was opening up all along the southern tip of Bataan. The area behind us re-echoed to the thud and crash of heavy gunfire. Grayish smoke puffs speckled Corregidor's sides. The Rock was blasting back at the Japs, but most of its shells were falling in the Mariveles region whence we had come.

At sundown we crossed Cabcaben airfield, from which our planes had taken off not thirty-nine hours before. Here again Jap artillery was going into action. We were marched across the field and halted inside a rice paddy beyond. We had had no food or water, and none was offered, but we were grateful of the opportunity to lie down on the earth and rest. The guards kept to the edges of the paddy, leaving us plenty of room.

I was just dropping off when there came an outburst of yelling and screeching. The Japs had charged in among us and were kicking us to our feet. They herded us back to the road and started marching us eastward again. During the brief respite leg muscles had stiffened. Walking was torture.

It was dark when we marched across Bataan field, which with Cabcaben field I had commanded two days before. It was difficult walking in the darkness. Now and again we passed the huddled forms of men who had collapsed from fatigue or had been bayoneted. I didn't kid myself that I was safe simply because I was keeping up the pace. I would not have been surprised at any time to feel a Jap blade slide between my ribs. The bloodthirsty devils now were killing us for diversion.

78

The march continued until about 10 P.M. When we were halted some naïve individual started a rumor that we were to be given water. Instead we were about-faced and marched back to the westward. For two more hours we stumbled over the ground we had just covered.

It was midnight when we recrossed Bataan field and kept going. We were within a short distance of Cabcaben field when the Japs diverted the line into a tiny rice paddy. There was no room to lie down. Some of us tried to rest in a half squat. Others drew up their knees and laid their heads on the legs of the men next to them. Jap guards stood around the edges of the little field, their feet almost touching the outer fringe of men.

I heard a cry, followed by thudding blows at one side of the paddy. An American soldier so tortured by the thirst that he could not sleep had asked a Jap guard for water. The Jap fell on him with his fists, then slugged him into insensibility with a rifle butt.

The thirst of all had become almost unbearable, but remembering what had happened to the colonel earlier in the day we asked for nothing. A Jap officer walked along just after the thirsty soldier had been beaten. He appeared surprised that we wanted water. However, he permitted several Americans to collect canteens from their comrades and fill them at a stagnant carabao wallow which had been additionally befouled by seeping sea water. We held our noses to shut out the nauseating reek, but we drank all the water we could get.

At dawn of the second day the impatient Japs stepped among and upon us, kicking us into wakefulness. We were hollow-eyed and as exhausted as we had been when we went to sleep. As we stumbled into the road we passed a Jap noncommissioned officer who was eating meat and rice.

"Pretty soon you eat," he told us.

The rising sun cast its blinding light into our eyes as we marched. The temperature rose by the minute. Noon came and went. The midday heat was searing. At 1 P.M. the column was halted and Jap noncoms told American and Fili-

79

pino soldiers they might fill their canteens from a dirty puddle beside the road. There was no food.

During the afternoon traffic picked up again. Troop-laden trucks sped past us. A grimacing Jap leaned far out, holding his rifle by the barrel. As the truck roared by he knocked an American soldier senseless with the gun's stock. Other Japs saw this and yelled. From now on we kept out of reach if we could. Several more American and Filipino prisoners were struck down.

At 2 P.M. we were told it would be necessary to segregate the prisoners as to rank; colonels together, majors together, and so on. This separated all units from their officers and afforded opportunity for another hour of sun treatment. There was no mention of food.

The line of march was almost due north now. We reached Balanga, about twenty miles from Cabcaben field, at sundown. We were marched into the courtyard of a large prison-like structure, dating to the Spanish days, and told we would eat, then spend the night there.

At one side of the yard food was bubbling in great caldrons. Rice and soy sauce were boiling together. Jap kitchen corpsmen were opening dozens of cans and dumping vienna sausage into the savory mess. The aromatic steam that drifted over from those pots had us almost crazy. While we waited we were given a little water.

We imagined the rice and sausages were for us, though we saw hundreds of ragged and sick Filipinos behind a barbed wire barricade near-by who had only filthy, fly-covered rice to eat. After drinking we were ordered into the line for what appeared to be a routine search. When it was finished an officer shouted something and the attitude of our guards swiftly changed.

They ordered us out of the patio and lined us up in a field across the road. As we left, grinning Japs held up steaming ladles of sausage and rice. The officer followed us to the field, then began stamping up and down, spouting denunciations and abuse. When he calmed enough to be understood. we heard this:

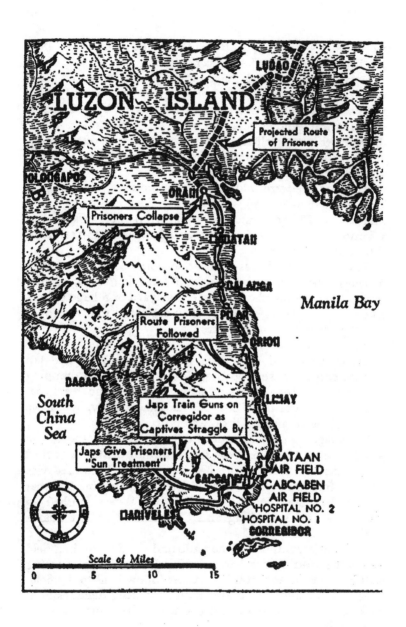

LUZON ISLAND

LUBAO

Projected Route
of Prisoners

OLONGAPO

ORANI

Prisoners Collapse

LIMATAN

BALANGA

Manila Bay

PILAR

Route Prisoners
Followed

ORION

DAGAS

South
China
Sea

LIMAY

Japs Train Guns on
Corregidor as
Captives Straggle By

Japs Give Prisoners
"Sun Treatment"

BATAAN
AIR FIELD

CABCABEN
AIR FIELD

HOSPITAL NO. 2

HOSPITAL NO. 1

BAGGANELLO

MARIVELES

CORREGIDOR

Scale of Miles

0   5   10   15

"When you came here you were told you would eat and be let to sleep. Now that is changed. We have found pistols concealed among three American officers. In punishment for these offenses you will not be given food. You will march to Orani (five miles to the north) before you sleep."

The accusation was a lie. If a pistol had been found, the owner would have been shot, beaten to death, or beheaded on the spot. Besides, we knew that the searchers hadn't overlooked even a toothbrush, to say nothing of a pistol. The Japs simply were adding mental torture to the physical. The Jap officer saw he wasn't believed. He did just what a Jap might be expected to do. Shortly after we resumed the march a staff car pulled up beside us.

Three American officers were dragged out of line and thrown into it. This in the words of Gilbert and Sullivan's Pooh Bah was "corroborative detail, intended to lend artistic verisimilitude to an otherwise bald and unconvincing narrative." We never saw the three officers again, though it is not hard to guess their fate. Men who had stood near two of them during the search said no guns had been found.

Our guards had been increased for the night march, and rigid discipline was imposed. We were formed into columns of fours. A new set of guards came up on bicycles and we were forced to walk practically at double quick to keep up. After two hours these guards were replaced by a group on foot who walked slowly with short mincing steps. The change of gait so cramped our leg muscles that walking was agony.

We had learned by rough experience that efforts to assist our failing comrades served usually to hasten their deaths and add to our own misery and peril. So we tried the next best thing—encouraging them with words. Talking had not been forbidden.

It was during a period of slow marching that an old friend, a captain in the medical corps, began dropping back through the ranks. Presently he was beside me. It was plain he was just about done in. I said:

"Hello, Doc. Taking a walk?"

82

"Ed," he said slowly, "I can't go another kilometer. A little farther and I'm finished."

"Well, Doc, I'm about in the same fix," I told him. Nothing more was said until we had covered two or three kilometers. Every now and then Doc would begin to lag a little. When this happened, the fellow on the other side of Doc would join me in slipping back some and giving him a little shove with our shoulders. He always took the hint and stepped up. At length he spoke again.

"I'm done, Ed. You fellows forget me and go on. I can't make another kilometer."

"I don't think I can either, Doc. I feel just about as you do."

That was the way we passed the night. Kilometer after kilometer crawled by, but Doc didn't fall out. If he had, his bones would be bleaching now somewhere along that road of death that led out of Bataan.

The hours dragged by and, as we knew they must, the drop-outs began. It seemed that a great many of the prisoners reached the end of their endurance at about the same time. They went down by twos and threes. Usually, they made an effort to rise. I never can forget their groans and strangled breathing as they tried to get up. Some succeeded. Others lay lifelessly where they had fallen.

I observed that the Jap guards paid no attention to these. I wondered why. The explanation wasn't long in coming. There was a sharp crackle of pistol and rifle fire behind us.

Skulking along, a hundred yards behind our contingent, came a "clean-up squad" of murdering Jap buzzards. Their helpless victims, sprawled darkly against the white of the road, were easy targets.

As members of the murder squad stooped over each huddled form, there would be an orange flash in the darkness and a sharp report. The bodies were left where they lay, that other prisoners coming behind us might see them.

Our Japanese guards enjoyed the spectacle in silence for a time. Eventually, one of them who spoke English felt he should add a little spice to the entertainment.

"Sleepee?" he asked. "You want sleep? Just lie down on road. You get good, long sleep!"

On through the night we were followed by orange flashes and thudding shots.

CHAPTER SIX

AT 3 A.M. OF APRIL 12, 1942—the second day after our sur-render—we arrived half dead at Orani, in northeastern Bataan, after a twenty-one-hour march from Cabcaben near the peninsula's southern tip. That thirty-mile hike over rough and congested roads had lasted almost from dawn to dawn.

It would have been an ordeal for well men. Added to the strength-sapping heat and blinding dust were the cruelties devised by the Jap guards. Considering our condition, I often wonder how we made it. We had had no food in days. Chronic exhaustion seemed to have possessed us. Many were sick. I know men who never could remember arriving at Orani. They were like Zombies—the walking dead of the Caribbean.

Near the center of the town the Japs ordered us off the road to a barbed wire compound a block away. It had been intended for five hundred men. Our party numbered more than six hundred. Already in it, however, were more than 1,500 Americans and Filipinos.

The stench of the place reached us long before we entered it. Hundreds of the prisoners were suffering from dysentery. Human waste covered the ground. The shanty that had served as a latrine no longer was usable as such.

Maggots were in sight everywhere. There was no room to lie down. We tried to sleep sitting up, but the aches of exhaustion seemed to have penetrated even into our bones.

Jap soldiers told us there would be rice during the morning. We paid no attention. We not only didn't believe them, we were too miserable to care. The sun came up like a blazing ball in a copper sky. With the first shafts of yellow light the temperature started up and, it seemed to me, the vile stench of the compound grew in intensity. Breathing the heavy heated air was physically painful.

I remember pondering that even if we had firearms none of us would be capable of using them. We were succumbing to the oriental tortures that subdue men, break their spirits, and reduce them below the level of animals.

As the sun climbed higher, Americans and Filipinos alike grew delirious. Their wild shouts and thrashings about dissipated their ebbing energy. They began lapsing into coma. For some it was the end. Starvation, exhaustion, and abuse had been too much for their weakened bodies. Brief coma was followed by merciful death. I had a blinding headache from the heat, glare, and stench. Several times I thought my senses were slipping.

When it was observed that men were dying, Japanese noncommissioned officers entered the compound and ordered the Americans to drag out the bodies and bury them. We were told to put the delirious ones into a thatched shed a few hundred feet away. When this had been done the grave digging began.

We thought we had seen every atrocity the Japs could offer, but we were wrong. The shallow trenches had been completed. The dead were being rolled into them. Just then an American soldier and two Filipinos were carried out of the compound. They had been delirious. Now they were in a coma. A Jap noncom stopped the bearers and tipped the unconscious men into the trench.

The Japs then ordered the burial detail to fill it up. The Filipinos lay lifelessly in the hole. As the earth began falling about the American, he revived and tried to climb out. His fingers gripped the edge of the grave. He hoisted himself to a standing position.

Two Jap guards placed bayonets at the throat of a Filipino

on the burial detail. They gave him an order. When he hesitated they pressed the bayonet points hard against his neck. The Filipino raised a stricken face to the sky. Then he brought his shovel down upon the head of his American comrade, who fell backward to the bottom of the grave. The burial detail filled it up.

For many of those who had been taken into the shade of the thatched shed the respite came too late. One by one their babblings ceased and their bodies twisted into the grotesque postures that mark a corpse as far as it can be seen.

During the long afternoon, stupor served as an anesthetic for most of the prisoners in the compound. There was no food. Toward evening the Japs allowed Americans to gather canteens and fill them at an artesian well. It was the first good water we'd had. Night brought relief from the heat, though there still was no room to lie down, despite the number of dead and delirious removed from the compound.

Dawn of April 13—our fourth day since leaving Mariveles —seemed to come in the middle of the night. Its magnificent colors and flaming splendor meant to us only the beginning of new sufferings. We averted our heads as the coppery light flooded our filthy prison. The temperature seemed to rise a degree a minute.

At 10 A.M., just as I was wondering how I could get through another day, there was a stir at the gates. Guards filed in and began lining us up in rows. Out of one of the dirty buildings came kitchen corpsmen, dragging cans of sticky gray rice which they ladled out—one ladleful to each man. Those of us who had mess kits loaned the lids to men who had none. There were not enough kits and lids to go around, so some of the prisoners had to receive their dole in cupped hands. The portion given each man was equivalent to a saucer or small plate of rice.

The food was unappetizing and was eaten in the worst possible surroundings, but it was eaten. Make no mistake about that. It was our first in many a day. I began feeling stronger immediately, despite the growing heat. There was not enough of the rice, however, to stay delirium and coma for the weaker prisoners. There were those for whom it came too late. Scenes of the previous afternoon were repeated. There were babblings and crazy shouts. There were additional burials in shallow graves.

The rest of us passed the afternoon in stupor. We continued to sit while the sun dropped behind the western mountains. In the twilight we were ordered to our feet. It still was light as we were marched out of the compound, toward the road. We looked at the artesian well, but the Japs warned us not to try to fill our canteens.

During the next four hours of marching we were tortured by the sound of bubbling water. Artesian wells lined the road. It seemed to me I could smell water. But we knew a bullet or a bayonet awaited the man who might try to reach the wells.

About midnight rain started falling. It was chilling, but it cleansed the filth from our stinging bodies and relieved the agony of parched dryness. Those with mess kits or canteen cups held them up toward the rain as they walked. The rain lasted about fifteen minutes and we shared the water with those who had no receptacles.

We were refreshed for a time, but as the grinding march continued men began falling down. The energy derived from the morning rice and the few swallows of rain water had been depleted. When I saw the first man go down I began counting the seconds. I wondered whether the Jap buzzard squad was following us as it had two nights before—the night of April 11.

A flash and the crack of a shot answered my question. The executioners were on the job to kill or wound mortally every prisoner who fell out of the marching line. All through the night there were occasional shots. I didn't count them. I couldn't.

Just before daybreak the guards halted the column and ordered us to sit down. I felt like a fighter who has been saved by the bell. The ground was damp and cool. I slept. Two hours later we were prodded into wakefulness and ordered to get up. The sun had risen.

Our course was northeasterly now and we were leaving the mountains and Bataan behind. The country in which we found ourselves was flat and marshy. There were small rivers and creeks and many rice paddies. This was Pampanga province.

I was somewhat refreshed by the rest, though walking now was much more difficult. Our stay on the damp ground had caused leg muscles to set like concrete. Even my bones seemed to ache. This was the cool of the morning, yet my throat still was afire with thirst.

And just across the road bubbled an artesian well. Its splashing was plainly audible and the clear water, glistening in the morning sun, was almost too much for my self-control. I thought once if I could reach that well and gulp all the water I wanted the Japs could shoot me and welcome. The next minute I told myself I was balmy even to entertain such a thought.

The Japs were aware of the well and they must have known what was passing through our minds. I have no doubt that they were expecting the thing that happened now. A Filipino soldier darted from the ranks and ran toward the well. Two others followed him. Two more followed these, then a sixth broke from the ranks.

Jap guards all along the line raised their rifles and waited for the six to scramble into the grassy ditch and go up on the opposite side, a few feet from the well. Most of the Filipinos fell at the first volley. Two of them, desperately wounded, kept inching toward the water, their hands outstretched. The Japs fired again and again, until all six lay dead. Thus did our fifth day of the death march start with a blood bath. I needed all the control I could muster.

Men had been murdered behind me all night, but the deeds had been veiled by darkness. There had been nothing to veil the pitilessness and wantonness of the murders I had just seen. I walked a long time with my head down and my

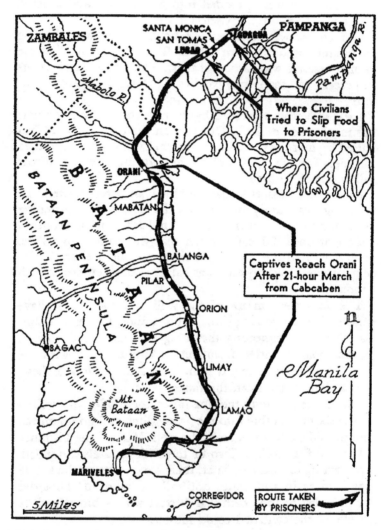

ZAMBALES

SANTA MONICA
SAN TOMAS
LUBAO

PAMPANGA

Mabolo R.

Pampanga R.

Where Civilians
Tried to Slip Food
to Prisoners

B A T A A N

BATAAN PENINSULA

ORANI

MABATANG

BALANGA

PILAR

Captives Reach Orani
After 21-hour March
from Cabcaben

ORION

BAGAC

LIMAY

Manila Bay

Mt. Bataan

LAMAO

MARIVELES

5 Miles

CORREGIDOR

ROUTE TAKEN
BY PRISONERS

fists clenched in my pockets, fighting to think of nothing at
all.

I was partly successful, enough so that from then on I prac-
ticed detaching myself from the scenes about me. I have no

89

doubt my cultivated ability to do this saved my sanity on more than one occasion in the days to come. I remember little of the two miles we walked after the six murders at the well. We were at the outskirts of Lubao, a sprawling city of 30,000, before mutterings about me brought me back to earth to look upon a new horror.

I saw that all eyes were directed toward an object hanging on a barbed wire fence that paralleled the road. It had been a Filipino soldier. The victim had been bayoneted. His abdomen was open. The bowels had been wrenched loose and were hanging like great grayish purple ropes along the strands of wire that supported the mutilated body.

This was a Japanese object lesson, of course. But it carried terrible implications. The Japs apparently had wearied of mere shootings and simple bayonetings. These had served only to whet the barbaric appetite. What might lie ahead for all of us we could only guess.

These thoughts still were in mind as our scarecrow procession began passing through the rough streets of Lubao. We were in a residential section. Windows of homes were filled with faces turned to us that bore compassionate expressions. News of our arrival raced down the street ahead of us.

Presently from the upper windows of a large house a shower of food fell among us. It was followed quickly by other gifts, tossed surreptitiously by sympathetic Filipinos who stood on the sidewalks. There were bits of bread, rice cookies, lumps of sugar and pieces of chocolate. There were cigarettes.

The Jap guards went into a frenzy. They struck out right and left at the Good Samaritans, slugging, beating, and jabbing bayonets indiscriminately. Japs tried to stamp on all the food that hadn't been picked up. They turned their rage upon us. When the townsfolk saw their gifts were only adding to our misery they stopped throwing them.

Some Filipinos asked the Jap officers if they might not help us. The petitioners were warned to stay away. I recall a merchant who wanted to open his store to us. We could have anything we wanted free, he said. A Jap officer denounced him, warned him to keep his distance. This was at San Tomas or Santa Monica, the two small settlements between Lubao and Guagua, about three miles to the northeast.

In Guagua the Filipino civilians also tried to slip food to us. For that they were beaten and clubbed—as we were. We passed through the hot streets without a halt.

Our next stop, just outside the city of Guagua, came near being a permanent one for me. At a long, muddy ditch we were allowed to dip up drinking water. After canteens had been filled I determined to soak my aching feet in the ooze at the ditch's edge. I was doing so when the order to resume the march was sounded unexpectedly. Putting on my shoes delayed me a few seconds.

I heard a guard shout in my direction, but I continued to struggle with the footgear. When I looked up the guard was raising his rifle. I snatched my shoes and plunged through the ditch toward the column of prisoners. I dodged from side to side with a prickling feeling all over my back. But the bullet didn't come. The guard probably would have missed—the Japs are bum shots—but I didn't think so then.

As I fell in step beside Doc, he pointed toward an officer just ahead of us. This was Captain Burt, who had given the alarm on our last night at Bataan field. He was eating a long sugar lump he had managed to secrete.

"I'm glad somebody got something," Doc said.

But in a minute or two Burt had dropped back beside us and was holding out the sugar. We each took a bite and tried to give it back. Burt shook his head.

"Split it, fellows," he said. "I've already had more than that."

I've never had such a quick reaction from anything. Strength flowed into me. I told Doc I felt as if I'd had a turkey dinner. This was an exaggeration, of course, but it illustrates what just a little food would have done for all of us. The Japs were starving us deliberately.

We neared San Fernando, Pampanga province, during the afternoon of our fifth day's march. It was at San Fernando, according to rumor, that we were to be put aboard a train and carried to a concentration camp.

From among the six hundred and more American and Filipino military prisoners who had started with me from Mariveles, many familiar faces were missing. We had come almost eighty-five miles with nothing to eat except the one ladle of rice given to us more than twenty-four hours before.

We had struck the railroad at Guagua and now could see the tracks which ran alongside the highway, amid the lush vegetation of the flat, marshy countryside. We could have entrained an hour before. I doubted, therefore, that the railroad figured in the Japs' plans for us. I was becoming certain that this was to be a march to the death for all of us. And the events of the next quarter hour did nothing to banish this belief.

Just ahead of me, in the afternoon heat, were two American enlisted men, stumbling along near the point of collapse. I wasn't in much better shape. At this moment we came abreast of a calasa [covered cart] which had stopped beside the road.

An American colonel who also had been watching the two enlisted men, observed that no Jap guard was near us. He drew the two soldiers out of line and helped them into the cart, then got in also. The Filipino driver tapped his pony. The cart had moved only a few feet when the trick was discovered.

Yammering Jap guards pulled the three Americans from the cart and dragged the Filipino from the driver's seat. A stocky Jap noncommissioned officer seized the heavy horsewhip. The enlisted men were flogged first. The crackling lash slashed their faces and tore their clothing. The searing pain revived them for a moment. Then they fell to the ground. The blows thudded upon their bodies. They lost consciousness.

The colonel was next. He stood his punishment a long time. His fortitude enraged the Jap, who put all his strength behind the lash. When the American officer finally dropped to his knees his face was so crisscrossed with bloody welts it was unrecognizable.

The trembling Filipino driver fell at the first cut of the

whip. He writhed on the ground. The lash tore his shirt and the flesh beneath it. His face was lacerated and one eye swollen shut. When the whipper grew weary, he ordered the driver on his way. The colonel, bleeding and staggering, was kicked back into the line of American prisoners.

I don't know what became of the enlisted men. I never saw them again. During the remaining two miles we marched to San Fernando I listened for shots, but heard none. The soldiers probably were bayoneted.

The sun still was high in the sky when we straggled into San Fernando, a city of 36,000 population, and were put in a barbed wire compound similar to the one at Orani. We were seated in rows for a continuation of the sun treatment. Conditions here were the worst yet.

The prison pen was jammed with sick, dying, and dead American and Filipino soldiers. They were sprawled amid the filth and maggots that covered the ground. Practically all had dysentery. Malaria and dengue fever appeared to be running unchecked. There were symptoms of other tropical diseases I didn't even recognize.

Jap guards had shoved the worst cases beneath the rotted flooring of some dilapidated building. Many of these prisoners already had died. The others looked as though they couldn't survive until morning.

There obviously had been no burials for many hours.

After sunset Jap soldiers entered and inspected our rows. Then the gate was opened again and kitchen corpsmen entered with cans of rice. We held our mess kits and again passed lids to those who had none. Our spirits rose. We watched as the Japs ladled out generous helpings to the men nearest the gate.

Then, without explanation, the cans were dragged away and the gate was closed. It was a repetition of the ghastly farce at Balanga. The fraud was much more cruel this time because our need was vastly greater. In our bewildered state it took some time for the truth to sink in. When it did we were too discouraged even to swear.

We put our mess kits away and tried to get some sleep. But

the Japs had something more in store for us. There was an outburst of shrill whooping and yelling, then the guards poured into the compound with fixed bayonets. They feinted at the nearest prisoners with the sharp points.

Those of us who were able rose to our feet in alarm. Evidently we did not appear sufficiently frightened. The Japs outside the compound jeered the jokesters within. One Jap then made a running lunge and drove his bayonet through an American soldier's thigh.

This stampeded several other prisoners who trampled the sick and dying men on the ground. Some prisoners tripped and fell and were trampled by their comrades. The Japs left, laughing. There was little sleep that night. The stench was almost unbearable. Hundreds of prisoners were kept awake by sheer weariness. There were shouts of delirium. There was moaning. There were the sounds of men gasping their last.

At dawn of April 15, 1942, the sixth day of our ordeal, we were kicked to our feet by Jap guards and ordered to get out of the compound. The Japs did not even make a pretense of giving us food or water. Our canteens had been empty for hours. Only muddy scum inside them reminded us that we had filled them at the ditch outside Guagua the afternoon before.

Enough prisoners had been brought out of the compound to form five companies of 115 men each. In this formation we were marched to a railroad siding several blocks away where stood five ancient, ramshackle boxcars. None of these could have held more than fifty men in comfort. Now 115 men were packed into each car and the doors were pulled shut and locked from the outside.

There was no room to move. We stood jammed together because there wasn't sufficient floor space to permit sitting. As the day wore on and the sun climbed higher the heat inside the boxcars grew to oven-like intensity. It was so hot that the air we breathed seemed to scorch our throats.

There was little ventilation, only narrow, screened slits at the ends of the cars. A large per cent of the prisoners was suffering from dysentery. The atmosphere was foul beyond

94

description. Men began to faint. Some went down from weakness. They lay at our feet, face down in the filth that covered the floor boards.

After a seemingly interminable wait the train started with a jerk. A jolting, rocking ride began. Many of the prisoners in the boxcar in which I stood were seized by nausea, adding to the vile state of our rolling cell. The ride lasted more than three hours. Later I heard that a number of men had died in each of the five cars. I don't know. I was too far gone to notice much at the journey's end.

When the doors were opened, someone, I can't remember who, said we had reached Capas, a town in Tarlac province, and that we were headed for O'Donnell prison camp—named for the town of O'Donnell.

When the prisoners tumbled out into the glaring sunlight the wretchedness of their condition brought cries of compassion from Filipino civilians who lined the tracks. The surly Jap guards silenced these sympathetic voices with stern warnings.

We were marched several hundred yards down the tracks to a plot of bare scorching ground amid the tropical undergrowth. It was another sun treatment. There was no breeze. The ground was almost too hot to touch. The heat dried the filth into our pores.

The Jap guards formed a picket wall around us to forestall the friendly Filipinos who had come to give us food and water. Some of these, however, hurled their offerings over the heads of the Japs, hoping they would fall into our midst. Then they took to the bush, outrunning the guards who pursued them.

We sat for two hours in the little clearing before the Japs ordered us to our feet. A seven-mile hike to O'Donnell prison was ahead of us. As we filed into the narrow dirt road that wound through the green walls of the jungle, it became obvious that more than a fourth of our number never would be able to make it.

We expected mass murder of those too weak to walk. Instead, the Jap officers indicated the stronger ones might assist

95

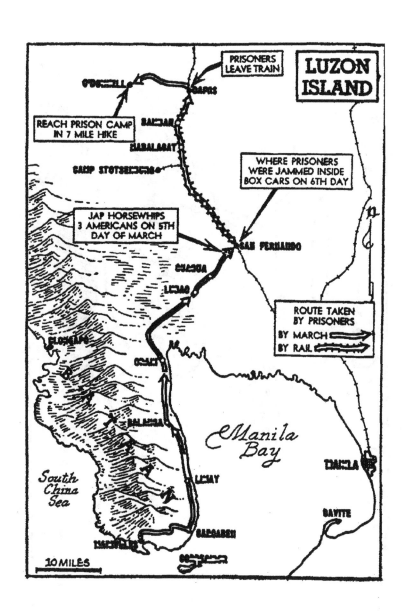

PRISONERS
LEAVE TRAIN

LUZON
ISLAND

O'DONNELL

CAPAS

REACH PRISON CAMP
IN 7 MILE HIKE

BAMBAN

MABALACAT

WHERE PRISONERS
WERE JAMMED INSIDE
BOX CARS ON 6TH DAY

CAMP STOTSENBURG

JAP HORSEWHIPS
3 AMERICANS ON 5TH
DAY OF MARCH

SAN FERNANDO

GUAGUA

LUBAO

ROUTE TAKEN
BY PRISONERS

BY MARCH

BY RAIL

FLORIDA

ORANI

BALANGA

Manila
Bay

MANILA

South
China
Sea

LIMAY

CAVITE

CABCABEN

MARIVELES

10 MILES

Lieutenant Colonel William Edwin Dyess

Officers' Mess at Bataan Field
Lt. Col. (then Capt.) Dyess second from end on left side of table.

Dyess Celebrates Raid
Capt. Dyess and Lt. "Lefty" Eades eat hot cakes cooked by the late
Brig. Gen. (then Col.) Harold H. George

Captain Dyess after His Bombing Raid in Subic Bay
(Bataan Field, March 3, 1942).

A Shelter near Bataan Field
Col. George in front of shack. Capt. Dyess lived in such a shelter
in the early spring of 1942.

Major General King and His Staff after Capture by the Japanese

Prisoners Being Disarmed by the Japanese at Mariveles

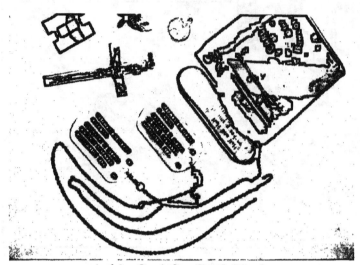

Articles Carried on Death March
Crucifix and other possessions of Lt. Col. Dyess. The tobacco can was his billfold.

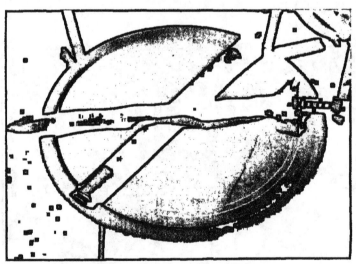

Dyess Trophy: a Moro Kris
This deadly weapon, brought back by Lt. Col. Dyess, is on display in his home town, Albany, Texas.

The Dyess Diary

In this diary was kept a day by day record of events
during the escape from the Japanese.

Captain Samuel C. Grashio

Capt. Grashio fought alongside Col. Dyess and escaped with him.
He holds a native Filipino dagger.

From:
~~William C. Dyess~~
William E. Dyess

Nationality ...American...

Rank ...Captain...

Camp Philippine Military Prison Camp No. 2,

To: Mrs. Marajen Stevick Dyess...

News Gazette...

Champaign, Illinois, USA.

IMPERIAL JAPANESE ARMY

1. I am interned at ...Philippine Military Prison Camp No. 2...

2. My health is — excellent, **good**, fair, poor.

3. I am — injured, sick in hospital; under treatment; **not under treatment**.

4. I am — improving; not improving; better; **well**.

5. Please see that my Government Insurance was converted in Oct.
    1941 .... is taken care of.

6. (Re: Family): I know you folks ... folks are all in OK. Do
    not worry about me. Keep your chin up darling. Love to U & ...

7. Please give my best regards to Mother, Jr., all Helen, & Friends.

A Message from the Prison Camp
Photostatic copy of first card sent, from Prison Camp No. 2, to Mrs. Dyess.

General MacArthur Greets Escaped Heroes

Left to right: Lt. Col. Dyess, Lt. Comdr M. H. McCoy,
Gen. MacArthur, Major S. M. Mellnik.

Dyess's Cablegram Announcing Escape

The Prison Food
Typical food provided in prison camps.

How He Downed a Jap Fighter
Lt. Col. Dyess shows Chris Meyer, in Champaign, Ill., how it was done.

Colonel Dyess in Hospital

Col. C. M. Beck, commander of military hospital at White
Sulphur Springs, with Lt. Col. Dyess.

Dyess Relates His Experiences

Other wounded officers in hospital listen to the Dyess story.

In the Summer of 1943

Mrs. Marajen Dyess (left), Mrs. Elizabeth Nell Denman, Dyess's sister, and Mrs. Vicellio at Champaign, Ill.

At White Sulphur

Photographer Swain Scalf, Mrs. Dyess, Col. Dyess, and Charles Leavelle.

the weaker ones. This was something new. There were precious few stronger ones, however.

As we straggled on we had ample reason to bless the kindly Filipinos of Capas. Having seen other prisoners pass that way, they had set out cans of water among the bushes and in high grass along the road.

The Japs found many of these and kicked them over before our eyes. But some were overlooked and a few of us were able to take the edge off our thirst. One gaunt American officer said he believed he owed his life to the good and thoughtful townfolk of Capas.

My first good look at O'Donnell prison was from atop a rise about a mile off. I saw a forbidding maze of tumbledown buildings, barbed wire entanglements, and high guard towers, from which flew the Jap flag.

I had flown over this dismal spot several times, but never had given it more than passing appraisal. I wondered as I looked at it now how long I would be there; how long I could last.

As we stood, staring dazedly, there came to me a premonition that hundreds about to enter O'Donnell prison this April day never would leave it alive. If I could have known what lay in store for us all, I think I would have given up the ghost then and there.

Sharp commands by the Jap guards aroused me. We started moving.

CHAPTER SEVEN

THE LONG LINE OF PRISONERS straggled through the eastern portal of O'Donnell prison camp, between high towers upon which were mounted machine guns. Gates in the barbed wire barricade closed behind us. Our guards marched us up a hill just south of the gate and seated us in the blazing sun near Japanese military headquarters.

We were given to understand we shortly would be "welcomed" by the enemy captain commanding the prison. During the searing forty-five-minute wait I studied the dismal reservation which stretched to the south, west, and north of the hill upon which we were seated.

The camp covered a wide area, probably several hundred acres. The road by which we had entered bisected it in the center. Lesser roads branched off to the north and south. The main road was flanked by barbed wire entanglements. The reservation was divided by similar barricades into several large square compounds.

In these were the unfinished and already dilapidated buildings that had been intended for use as a Filipino military establishment. Work had been abandoned at the start of the war.

The northwestern section now had been set aside for air forces, prisoners learned. Just east of this, prisoners from the tank corps were together.

The northeast section had been allotted to prisoners from the coast artillery. A sluggish, muddy stream snaked its way across the camp, entering from the east and wandering westward until it reached the tank corps compound, where it turned to flow in a southerly direction.

I was taking all this in when there arose a babble of high-pitched voices from our Jap guards and we had to stand up for a search. On the march from Bataan all our personal possessions had been taken from us. We had nothing left except our United States army blankets, which we had carried from Mariveles. These now were taken away and we sat down again to wait for the Jap captain.

Finally he appeared: a gnarled, misshapen creature, as grotesque as anything supposedly human I ever have looked upon. We learned he had been retired, but had been called back to duty at the start of the war.

He had squint eyes. He roared at us with a pomposity

reminiscent of Mussolini's. But the loose-lipped vacuity of his expression was that of an idiot. The captain mounted a low platform and stared at us. Beside the dais stood a fat Filipino-Japanese boy, holding a straw hat in both his pudgy hands.

At length, the captain began to speak. After each long burst of gibberish the fat interpreter translated for us in a purring, lackadaisical monotone while the captain glared up and down our ranks.

"The captain, he say Nippon has capture Javver [sic], Sumatter, and New Guinyah," the fat boy said. "Captain, he say we soon have Austrayler and New Zealyer."

The interpreter stepped back while the Jap captain yelled at us again.

"The captain, he say America and Nippon enemies," the interpreter continued. "Always will be enemies. If Nippon do not defeat America this time, Nippon fight again and again until America defeated. Always will be war until America is Nippon's."

And now came the part of the "welcome" which was of most significance to us. The captain delivered it with particular violence, but it came to us in the interpreter's sibilant whisper:

· "Captain, he say you not prisoners of war. You are sworn enemies of Japan. Therefore, you will not be treated like prisoners of honorable war. Captain, he say you will be treated like captives. He say you do not act like soldiers. You got no discipline. You do not stand at attention while he talk. Captain, he say you will have trouble from him."

It is true that in our state of hunger, thirst, and fatigue, many of us had paid little attention to the harangue. Some, indeed, actually had their backs turned toward this agent of the Son of Heaven. As to his threats of trouble, we figured he would have to be a genius to cause us any more trouble than we had had. The captain now was demanding that our commanding officer be pointed out. We didn't bother to answer.

The interpreter spoke rapidly to the captain, explaining, as we later learned, that we were remnants of many organiza-

99

tions; that no officer was in charge. The captain glared at us a while longer, then stepped down and strutted away, followed by the waddling interpreter who still held his straw hat in both hands. The guards lined us up and we marched from the hill to the tumbledown buildings in the northernmost section of the camp.

Our first thoughts were of water, to drink and to bathe in. But there was very little. In our section of the camp there was only one faucet. The water was piped from a well across the road. The well's asthmatic gasoline pump broke down every hour or so and was out of commission usually for two or three.

We stood in line in the glare and heat, waiting to fill our canteens with tepid water. This eased our thirst somewhat, but we all were so dehydrated we could have drunk a gallon and still have felt need for more. Even our pores cried out for cool, clear water.

Soon afterward we each got one mess kit of rice. There was no bread, meat, or fruit. Except for the ladle of rice at Orani and two bites of sugar on the road, this was my first food in six days of marching. It developed later that some of the American prisoners were kept on the road in the heat and dust as long as twelve days. Casualties among them were very high.

With twenty-two other officers of the air forces I was assigned to a ramshackle structure fourteen feet wide and twenty feet long. The unfinished roof was open in the center, admitting the burning sunshine and the rain. There were neither cots nor mats. We pulled grass and weeds to lie on in dry weather. When it rained we crawled under the flooring.

There were no lights in the barracks, but there were plenty around the camp at night. Searchlights at Jap headquarters and atop the towers were trained along the barbed wire. Walking patrols were abroad at all times. Escape seemed impossible. A delirious soldier, who got out somehow, was flogged unmercifully and tied up by the wrists in the sun in front of headquarters.

The next day he was put into an open compound from

which he also escaped. After the Japs seized him he was flogged within an inch of his life. Torn and bleeding, he again was exposed to the sun all day. He disappeared on the following night. We never saw him again, but we know he didn't escape.

When I began to get about the camp a little, I found that the quarters we had thought so miserable really were luxurious as compared to those provided some of the men. Many had no shelter whatever.

When we had been at O'Donnell about a week, the daily death rate among the Americans was twenty a day. Filipinos were dying at a rate of 150 a day. In two weeks fifty Americans were dying each day. The Filipino death toll had soared to 350 each twety-four hours.

The burial problem was serious. It was difficult to find men strong enough to dig graves. Regulation burial was unknown. Shallow trenches had to serve. Into these ten or twelve bodies were dumped—often without identification tags—and covered by a thin layer of earth.

Many new prisoners arrived daily. Most of them were sick and all were in varying stages of starvation. The disintegrating building that passed as a hospital soon was packed. Men were laid shoulder to shoulder on the bare floor. There were no blankets. Many of the sick and dying were naked.

When all floor space had been taken, the patients were laid out on the ground beneath the floors. The stench of the place was beyond description.

The Japs provided no medicine. American doctors who were prisoners in the camp were given no instruments, medicines, or dressings. They were not allowed sufficient water to wash the human waste from the sick and dying men. When all "hospital" space was gone many American soldiers lay out in the open, near the latrines, until they died.

In the early days of our stay at O'Donnell there were no latrines or other sanitary facilities. There were flies by the millions. They droned all day long, settling alternately upon the filth, then upon the containers of gray rice the Japs issued to the prisoners. When the Japs at last issued shovels for digging latrines, most of the men were too weak to use them.

Starvation was everywhere. Men who had weighed two hundred pounds or so now weighed ninety or less. Every rib was visible. They were living skeletons, without buttocks or muscle. On seeing a man lying asleep it was difficult to say whether he was alive or dead.

We hadn't the strength to move about much. My only walking was done on trips to the hospital to visit the men of the 21st Pursuit Squadron. I found one of my technical sergeants on the floor. He was naked and covered with defecation and flies. There were sores on his body—evidence of the violence he had done himself while delirious—and there was no antiseptic.

When I found him he was unable to drink water, eat rice, or recognize his friends. While on Bataan this man had weighed 185 pounds. When he died—soon after I came upon him—I doubt that he weighed ninety.

Another man from the 21st had been stuffed beneath a building. His condition was about the same as that of the first. This time, however, I was able to buy for five dollars a small, flat tin of fish from a Jap soldier and we thought we could save our friend. We stole water and washed him, then moved him into a building and covered him with a blanket.

We fed him the fish, mixed with rice. But it was too late. He died the next day.

The most common causes of death at O'Donnell were malaria, dysentery, and beriberi, none of them necessarily fatal if even elementary care is provided. Many of us were afflicted with all three of these at once. Mosquitoes descended upon us in clouds. Few of the prisoners had blankets, mosquito nets, or any other protection.

Frequently, when they were inspecting the wretched area, the Japs promised us medicines. They never delivered them, except on one occasion when the Red Cross was permitted to send in quinine from Manila for malaria patients. We never learned how much was sent. Though thousands were sick and dying of malaria, the Japs issued just enough quinine to take care of about ten cases.

Suffering was worst among the hundreds afflicted with beri-beri, a disease resulting from a deficiency of vitamins in the diet. Feet, ankles, and legs were swollen almost double normal size. Faces were puffed up like balloons.

When the condition affected the heart, death followed quickly. There is no need here to describe the anguished deaths of the dysentery victims.

In our first week at O'Donnell camp the Japs began impressing American and Filipino prisoners into labor gangs despite the appalling physical condition to which they had been reduced by starvation, disease, and lack of medical attention.

Each day the Jap guards led out the details of men, half of whom were unable to stand, let alone work. Oftener than not, these men failed to return in the evenings. There were deaths by the dozens in the barracks each night. And these were men the Japs contended were physically able to work.

The prisoners were organized into companies of two hundred each with an American officer at its head. The officers went along with the men, but were not allowed to supervise the work. If we could have assigned the men to the tasks, sparing the enfeebled soldiers and shifting the heavier work to the stronger ones, we might have been able to save many lives.

But we were used chiefly as interpreters and as butts for the jokes, insults, and abuse of the Japs. By May 15, a month after our internment at O'Donnell, less than twenty men of each company were able to go on detail and not many of these were able to labor in the equatorial sun.

For those unable to go on detail the Japs had another treatment. Regardless of physical condition they were lined up, each time when the heat was greatest, supposedly to stand inspection.

Most of these inspections never came off. At other times the Japs would pretend to count us. The idea was to keep the prisoners standing as long as possible in the glaring heat. Many collapsed and died.

In the two months we spent at O'Donnell more than 2,200

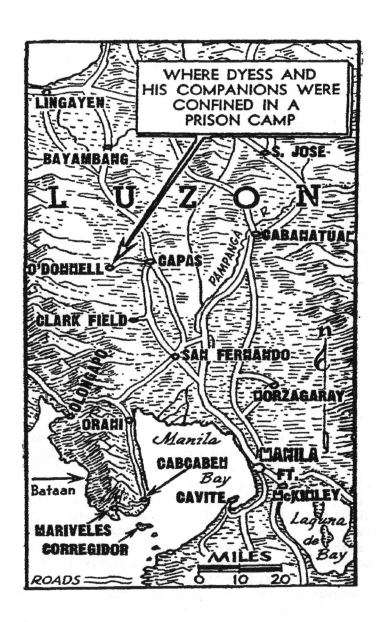

WHERE DYESS AND
HIS COMPANIONS WERE
CONFINED IN A
PRISON CAMP

LINGAYEN

BAYAMBANG

S. JOSE

L U Z O N

CABANATUAN

PAMPANGA R.

O'DONNELL

CAPAS

CLARK FIELD

OLONGAPO

SAN FERNANDO

NORZAGARAY

ORANI

Manila

CABCABEN

MANILA

FT.

Bay

Bataan

CAVITE

McKINLEY

MARIVELES

Laguna

CORREGIDOR

de

Bay

MILES

ROADS

0   10   20

American war prisoners died. The Filipino death toll was many times this. Most of the deaths were caused by disease bred of mosquitoes, filth, heat, and abuse. But if the Japs had allowed us just a little more food I am convinced there would have been far fewer deaths.

The Philippines were a land of plenty. In addition to their own food supply, brought with them when they invaded, the Japs had vast stores captured from the Americans and had access to the bountiful natural food resources of the islands. Therefore, the conclusion is inescapable that the Japs deliberately had set out to starve us.

Our diet was chiefly rice, served three times a day. The Japs gave us meat twice in two months. Neither time was there enough to flavor our watery soup. On these two occasions less than a fourth of the men got any meat to eat and the portion for those who did was one piece, less than an inch square.

Once in a while they gave us inferior sweet potatoes. Many of these were too rotten to eat. Nevertheless, it was necessary to post guards at the garbage dumps to prevent starving men from eating those that had been thrown away. The sweet potato ration per man was usually one spoonful.

Until the last of our stay at O'Donnell there were no knives with which to peel the potatoes. They were boiled with their skins on and mashed with a two-by-four timber in a fifty-five-gallon oil drum.

Occasionally we were given mango beans, a kind of cow pea. These were considered a great delicacy. A spoonful of beans plus some of the watery soup in which they had been cooked helped make a tasty meal when poured over rice.

Once or twice there was flour, which we mixed with bean juice to make a pasty gravy. The issues of coconut lard—practically our only protein—totaled one teaspoonful for the two months. A little food trickled through from the American and British Red Cross, but the parcels the Japs permitted to reach us were scanty in relation to our needs.

Japanese authorities forbade outside purchases by those who had managed to secrete their money. As a result, Jap soldiers set up an intramural black market. The tiny tin of fish which we purchased for five dollars for our dying squadron mate was typical of the goods and prices in the black market.

The filth that pervaded the camp was not absent in the kitchens. These were shacks with dirt floors. They hummed with flies and mosquitoes. There were no cleaning facilities. Each American kitchen was provided with two cauldrons, a shovel for scooping up rice, and the fifty-five-gallon drum already mentioned. There was no water for washing these utensils or the food.

There was water only for cooking and drinking. I was in O'Donnell prison thirty-five days before I had a bath—in one gallon of stolen water. My clothing was unchanged and unwashed for six weeks.

The stream that meandered through the reservation was befouled from the dysentery epidemic. Delirious men had to be restrained forcibly from drinking its vile waters. Several Filipinos eluded the self-appointed guards, drank from the stream, and were dead in a few days.

During the last ten days at O'Donnell the rains came, flushing out the little waterway. We washed our clothing and bathed—without soap, of course. No razors were allowed in camp, so we had long straggly beards.

Our talk and thoughts were almost continually of food; food we had enjoyed in the past, food we craved now, and food we intended to enjoy upon our release. At first I wanted steaks; big Hereford steaks from Shackelford county, Texas. Then my fancy settled upon eggs. I wanted them fried and by the platter.

Each night as I lay down to sleep I was tortured by this craving. I dreamed of them. Sometimes it seemed I was wallowing in Gargantuan plates of eggs, smashing the yellows and absorbing them through my pores.

As it always is in dreams, I never could taste or smell the eggs. Invariably I awakened, madder than hell and hungrier than before. When a man actually is starving he loses all desire for food and merely grows weaker and weaker. The artful Japs gave us just enough food to keep us in an agony of hunger at all times.

Our talks about food sometimes almost drove us crazy. I recall one agonizing session that had to do with chocolate milkshakes. I said if I could have all the thick milkshakes I could drink I would give five hundred dollars for them. This seemed to hit the spot with the others. Our misery descended to new depths.

There was little talk about the folks at home. Our thoughts of them we kept bottled up within ourselves. When I thought of my parents, my sister, and my wife I always calculated the time of day where they were.

This was done by subtracting twenty-four hours from Manila time and adding eight hours. This gave me San Francisco time. Addition of two more hours gave me central war time, which is observed at Albany, Tex., and Champaign, Ill., the homes of my loved ones. But I never mentioned them to the other fellows.

Some of the men became more and more reticent and eventually ceased to talk at all. A captain in our immediate group would allow days to pass without uttering a syllable. Another captain talked incessantly to anyone who would listen and to himself. He had been strafed and bombed repeatedly. The doctors said he was demented.

As is always true of men cast away in adversity, we began to think a great deal of religion. This was chiefly in our minds and souls, however. There was little surface indication of the trend except for Bible reading. A few Testaments had been smuggled into the camp and the Red Cross had sent in a few.

During the entire time I was in Japanese prisons I never saw an idle Bible. In the daylight hours those little volumes were being read constantly. You never saw men on their knees at prayer, either singly or in groups. But there was a very definite communion between ourselves and God.

In the early days at O'Donnell prison the Japs forbade us to hold divine services. Later the Protestant and Catholic chaplains who, like ourselves, were prisoners of war, renewed their appeals and permission was granted.

Protestant services were held outdoors each Sunday in the early morning, before the sun grew too hot. The fellows sat on the ground around the chaplain. They sang a few hymns everyone knew. The sermons impressed me greatly. They were simple, yet solid. Oratory and what is known as "pulpit personality" were absent.

The chaplains spoke to us as God might have; simply and directly. A lot of us embraced religion, but it was not a whooping and hollering religion. We prayed, silently. I asked for help and strength and for forgiveness when I felt I had transgressed or had shirked my duty as a Christian.

I never thought of God or addressed Him as a distant, awesome being somewhere in the sky. I felt much closer to Him than that. It may seem strange to some, but I thought of Him as "The Old Man" —the affectionate, respectful title soldiers apply to a commanding officer.

When it was necessary to take a long chance I would say to myself: "I have nothing to worry about. The Old Man will see me through."

I was brought up a Presbyterian and had been taught predestination and fatalism, but it was a Jap bullet that crystallized these teachings into belief. I was over the enemy lines in a P-40 when a slug came up from below, knocked off part of my radio set, and zinged out through the top of the plane. If I hadn't been leaning over to look out the left side of the cockpit it would have caught me just back of the chin and have plowed upward into my brain.

I thought about this a great deal when I got down. What prank of fate had saved me from that bullet? I decided it could have been only one thing: it simply had not been my day to get it.

When I had pursued that line of thought to its conclusion I was a fatalist. This fortified me in the last days of Bataan and through the tragic days I spent in Japanese prisons.

We had just begun to look forward to the Sunday services when the Japs ordered them discontinued. After a couple of weeks, however, the ban was lifted.

The Catholic boys attended mass in one of the prison

buildings. There was no altar, the priests having to use benches or whatever was available. There were, of course, no candles or vestments.

The Japs allowed the priests enough flour to make the thin, unleavened wafers or Hosts used in Holy Communion. In camps where we later were confined, the priests were supplied with vestments by the International Red Cross. The Japs in the other camps permitted construction of altars.

None of us ever was able to understand why the Japs allowed us the solace of religion. It was a strange departure from their policy of inhumanity. There probably was a selfish reason. Maybe they thought religion would soften us. If they figured that way they figured wrong.

The worst jolt I got at O'Donnell prison camp came soon after we had arrived. On one stiflingly hot morning a Japanese officer stepped into our barracks.. He called out my name and the name of another man.

I had expected to be questioned by Japanese intelligence officers, but the thing that shocked me was the other name the Jap called. It was that of the captain beheaded on Mariveles airfield at the start of the Death March.

Why we should have been summoned together I couldn't understand. The captain, of course, didn't answer. As I walked up the hill with the Jap I was nervous.

At Japanese military headquarters I was halted in front of a desk occupied by a thin-faced, intelligent looking officer. Beside the Jap sat a Filipino captain who seemed to have been pressed into service as an interpreter. It was quickly apparent, however, that the Jap knew more English than he was likely to let on.

He asked at once for the other man. I said that so far as I had been able to learn he never had reported at O'Donnell. The Jap made a note upon a dossier. I then saw he had a dossier for me. My name had been typewritten at the top, but the rest of the document was in Japanese.

I grew more worried. How much did they think they knew about me? The next question reassured me somewhat.

"What do you do with 21st Pursuit Squadron?"

"I was a pilot," I told him.

"Only a pilot?"

"Only a pilot."

"Not officer?"

I said, "No." He was suspicious and I wondered if he could have known I was squadron commander. He appeared to be satisfied for the moment about my status with the 21st Pursuit. He then wanted to know about our airfields and our "hidden planes."

I told him there were no hidden planes; that they all had been shot down. He knew the airfields as well as I did, so I named them off for him. He asked about radio and air alarm service. I told him I knew only about the radio in our planes.

After each question and answer the Jap would look at me keenly and ask abruptly:

"And you only a pilot? Not officer?"

"Only a pilot," I would say, as cheerfully as possible.

His questions covered practically everything. How fast would our planes fly? That, I told him, depended upon the condition of the plane; sometimes very fast, sometimes not so fast.

How far could our radios send and from how far could they receive? Well, that depended upon conditions. Sometimes very far; sometimes not so far.

How far in miles, usually? Two miles, as a usual thing, but occasionally as far as thirty.

The Jap was getting nettled.

The Filipino captain undoubtedly saw I was giving the Jap the runaround, though he never let on. He could have helped him out several times. I began to feel a little better. I was told, however, to be back the next day for "new questions."

I didn't like the sound of that. I figured he intended to do a little investigating. Apparently he was not able to, because his questions the next day all had to do with radio. I told him I knew nothing about codes. I was strictly a flier, I said, and had nothing to do with communications.

"You go back," the Jap said. "There is communications officers in camp. You go find and bring back here tomorrow."

Back in our compound I looked up a young lieutenant who had been communications officer in our squadron. His name was Leroy. I told him about the grilling. I asked him if he would like to take a swing at a little questioning. He said he surely would. The next day we were escorted up the hill together.

The kid was a whiz. He started shooting technical data at the Jap officer at a great rate. His words didn't make sense. The Jap soon was so befuddled he had to appeal to the Filipino captain, who threw up his hands and said in effect that it was too deep for him.

When our inquisitor had taken five or six pages of notes in Japanese he gave it up and turned back to me. He wanted to know the complete setup of an American air squadron; officers, technicians, crew—everything. And he wanted a diagram of it. He got one.

When, finally, I had finished covering a large sheet of paper with labeled squares and circles, connected by lines, the chart was so confusing it looked almost like the real thing. I was proud of it. Leroy and I were dismissed and the last I saw of the Jap intelligence officer he was looking hopelessly and with furrowed brow from my diagram to Leroy's radio data and back to the diagram. I wasn't bothered again.

CHAPTER EIGHT ·

IT MAY SEEM RIDICULOUS, but in the face of all our adversities, we continued hopeful and optimistic during the first month of captivity. Indeed, there were many of us who never despaired of regaining our freedom, even though hope after hope was blighted.

In the early days our faith and wishful thinking were centered upon Corregidor. Rumors trickled through that the Rock was taking a terrible pounding from artillery on Bataan and from the Japanese air force. Our guards would tell us nothing, but day in and day out we could see and hear the heavy bombers as they passed in the vicinity of O'Donnell, en route to and from Corregidor. We knew that so long as they continued to go and return we could be sure the Rock still was holding out.

We had no hope that the Corregidor garrison eventually would launch a counterinvasion and rescue us. That was out of the question. But there were definite reasons why our spirits should rise with each additional day the fortress held out. One was that the Japs might consider the extended siege too costly in time, men, and matériel, and offer generous surrender terms that would include us. We later were to hear rumors that just such a thing had come to pass.

Another reason for hope was that if Corregidor could hold the Japs at bay long enough, the aroused American people might demand that a force be sent to rescue the gallant defenders and that the rescue would include us.

We didn't think for one minute that we had been abandoned to our fate, even though some of the fellows did sing snatches of the malicious song that went something like this:

"We are the orphans of Bataan,
"No mama, no papa, and no Uncle Sam!"

We were sure Uncle Sam was coming after us. It was just a matter of how soon. Thus we continued to hope. And when immediate hopes collapsed, we always could fall back on that nebulous one of possible escape from the prison camp, the possible theft of a sailing canoe, and possible arrival at Australia or some other friendly haven.

And there came the day, of course, when the number of bombers passing over was greatly reduced. This was on May 7 or 8. The next day there were fewer still. Then only one or two came over and, at length, none at all. There was a silence of many days. Word trickled in through Filipinos that the Rock had surrendered. Beyond that we could learn nothing.

It was during the third week in May that the rumors began to flood into our prison by the hundreds. Most of them were too fantastic for even the most wishful of us to credit. There were others, however, that could have had a foundation of truth. It was upon these that we lived.

One of the better ones was to the effect that the Rock's surrender had contained a provision for sending home all the survivors of Corregidor, Bataan, and the southern islands. You will say this simply didn't make sense. But consider that nothing the Japs had done thus far had made sense.

Consider, too that this report was followed by another from a pretty solid source, which said the steamer *Blackhawk* was in Manila bay being painted white for the transfer of prisoners to the United States. And on the heels of this, a Filipino smuggled in a package of cigarettes containing a note which read: "Be brave. You will soon be free."

I saw the note. I can't say I really believed it, but I stopped throwing cold water on the hopes of others who were in much worse condition than I and who gleaned from these notes enough encouragement to keep on living. To say that many of our men actually kept alive on these hopes is no exaggeration.

It was just after seeing the cigarette package note that I heard one of the technicians from my squadron was down at the hospital. He was a man who knew just about all there was to know about airplane mechanism. He had weighed two hundred pounds when Bataan fell; a magnificent physical specimen. Yet that day at the hospital I passed him without recognition. I walked to the end of the row and was returning when I heard my name called in a husky whisper

I looked at the speaker a full minute before I identified him. He was a bundle of bones and sagging, yellowed flesh. He couldn't have weighed more than eighty pounds. I saw at a glance that he was finished. It was too late for food. There was nothing I or any of us could do. I knelt beside him on the filthy floor.

"Ed," he whispered, "what do you think of these rumors that are going around?"

I knew then that I believed none of them, just as I knew he never would see home again. But the hope that glimmered in his eyes was too much for me. You can see the same look in the eyes of homeless, hungry puppies that think they have found a friend. I couldn't tell him. I said as cheerfully as I could:

"I don't know what you've heard, but those reports about the Japs wanting to send us home and the *Blackhawk* being painted white for the trip sound mighty good to me."

"Do they, Ed? Sure enough?"

"Sure enough, boy. They do. I'm banking on getting home. But you've got to pull yourself together and begin to get strong so they'll let you go and not keep you here for treatment."

He really brightened up. He said he would do whatever I told him. Our talk had made a new man of him, he told me. That boy died the next morning.

And within a few days the hopes of those who had believed the rumors died also. The prisoners from Corregidor began coming in. There were not many of them. Most of the 10,000 who had surrendered were sent to Cabanatuan prison camp, several miles to the east of O'Donnell. From those who did come to our camp we learned the details of the Rock's surrender and what followed. It was a story of Japanese treachery and ruthlessness that paralleled our own experiences.

I tell Corregidor's story here because, like our own, it was withheld for a long time by military authorities and because I heard it first hand from men in whose minds it remained vivid in all its horror. I have said that I heard the opening cannonade as we marched out of Bataan on April 10. This continued, fairly steadily, until the last week in April. Then the Japs doubled and tripled the intensity of their fire, keeping it up day and night and augmenting the artillery bombardment by heavy bomber raids from morning to night. How many thousands of projectiles and bombs exploded on and in Corregidor never will be known.

At this time, it should be remembered, American forces still were holding out in the southern islands. The snakish rage of the Japanese had been directed particularly at these forces and at Corregidor because when General King surrendered Bataan, he had refused to surrender the Rock and the southern garrisons on the ground that General Wainwright was chief in command and that only Wainwright could act for the others.

In the first days of May the relentless hammering knocked out the last of Corregidor's major batteries. After dark of May 5 the Japs laid down a devastating artillery barrage to cover their landing parties. The Rock's garrison waged a desperate and gallant defense, taking a staggering toll of the invaders. But the rain of shells was too much. The Japs landed in numbers. Shortly before dawn Corregidor's plight was hopeless. It was decided to surrender as soon as matériel, stores, and such naval vessels as remained could be destroyed.

In the last hours, thousands of dollars in American currency were fed to the flames to keep it out of the Japanese war treasury. Wireless sets, air warning systems, the remaining ordnance, and coding paraphernalia were smashed. The surrender was effected and the horde of Jap soldiers swarmed through the tunnels of the Rock, looting and wrecking.

This, however, was a minor irritation. The merciless shelling and bombing had ended, and in the silence that pervaded the galleries and tunnels of Corregidor taut nerves began slowly to relax.

But behind the scenes, General Wainwright and his staff were engaged in a stormy session with the Japanese commanders, who demanded that Wainwright order the surrender of the three generals in the southern islands. Wainwright argued in vain he had no control over them. The Japanese, who had been civil, even courteous, at first, now delivered their ultimatum. Unless all American and Filipino forces surrendered at once, the 10,000 Corregidor prisoners would be massacred. Apparently Wainwright believed the Japs were bluffing. He refused to yield.

On the morning of May 7 the eighteen-hour respite ended.

The silence that had hung over the Rock and lower Bataan was shattered by the crash of heavy artillery, fire, the roar of motors and explosions of shells and bombs. The Rock, utterly defenseless now, was getting it again.

The prisoners to whom I talked were convinced this was done to show General Wainwright the Japs were not bluffing; that death awaited the Corregidor captives unless all demands were met.

There were reports that the Jap command had forced General Wainwright to view the attack and that he was an unwilling watcher as the 10,000 prisoners were marched out of the fortress and installed in the 92nd Field Garage area where, it was announced, they would remain until all American resistance ceased or until time for their own executions.

There were no latrines. The area soon became unspeakably filthy. There was only one water hydrant for these thousands of men and the Japs sent no water from the outside. During the first week there was no food except the bits prisoners had been able to smuggle in on their persons. After that there were doles of rice once a day, sometimes with a watery vegetable broth.

From dawn to dark the heat was stupefying. The Japs at first refused to permit the prisoners to cool off in the sea, which washed one side of the internment area, but when they saw that the shallow waters had become fouled with the filth that covered the compound, they amusedly let the prisoners go in.

The men of Corregidor well knew the seriousness of their plight. As no word came to assure them General Wainwright would accede to the Jap terms, they began to look upon each dawning day as possibly their last. They were under no illusions.

The General, meanwhile, appealed to the American southern commanders to surrender "in the name of humanity." There were reports that he followed up by sending members of his staff as messengers to renew the appeal in person.

Within a few days the surrenders began. The last to yield was Major General William F. Sharp, whose forces thirty miles north of Davao had controlled the island of Mindanao. He surrendered on May 11.

A little more than a week later the Corregidor prisoners were informed they no longer were hostages; that they would be taken to internment camps on Luzon island as prisoners of war. Just at sundown they were crowded aboard three freighters for transfer across the bay to Manila. The ships did not move until morning, however, and the wretched Americans and their Filipino comrades spent a night of misery.

When it grew light the steamers got under way. They passed up Manila, however, and dropped anchor below the city. Landing barges came alongside, and the prisoners were loaded into these. They made trip after trip, always stopping several yards from shore while the guards forced the Americans overboard in water neck deep.

As the last of the bedraggled captives pulled themselves ashore, the sun reached the zenith. No time was allowed for rest. They were ordered to march. In the hours that followed they plodded up and down the streets of Manila, exposed to the sneers and abuse of Jap soldiers. The Filipino civilians—for whom the show had been staged—saw nothing glorious or even funny in the plight of the captured soldiers. There were looks and even cries of compassion.

After the first few miles, exhausted prisoners began falling to the ground. The guards pricked them with short jabs of the bayonet until they got up again or until it was established they were unconscious. If insensible, the victims were loaded into trucks. One of those who collapsed was an army colonel. He died without regaining consciousness. After the march the prisoners spent the night in Old Bilibid prison. On the day following they were started for the internment camps. The great majority went to Cabanatuan and when we of the 21st Pursuit Squadron were transferred there I met many friends.

The arrival of the Corregidor prisoners added to crowded conditions at O'Donnell. Most of them had no shelter, even though death had reduced O'Donnell's population by many hundreds. When the rains came soon after this, deaths increased among the more weakened captives. Men huddled together beneath the filthy, sagging floors for warmth.

The daily downpours did some good, however. They flooded our compound, cleansing the earth and flushing out the little stream. It washed our bodies and supplied us with an abundance of drinking water. Those who were fairly strong benefited. But because of the rising death toll they could take no joy in the physical relief thus afforded.

As the rains slackened, there were rumors that some of the American prisoners were to be transferred to Cabanatuan, several miles to the eastward. This was some official confirmation, so we got ready.

During the last days at O'Donnell I was chosen to accompany a detail being sent to Clark field—the old home of the 21st Pursuit Squadron. We were to clean up the wreckage in preparation for Jap soldiers who were to arrive later in the day.

When they came they let us pretty well alone. One officer, however, whose rank was equivalent to that of an American first lieutenant, seemed to take a liking to me and made me follow him around the rest of the day. He had fought at Singapore, in China, and on Bataan. He spoke some English and with the few Jap words I knew we could talk quite well.

He was proud of his sword, which he repeatedly pulled half out of its scabbard. Each bit of conversation ended with this gesture. Then he would say:

"Japanese soldier very brave; very good. American soldier no good."

I always would reply: "American soldiers on Bataan very, very hungry."

"Yaah!" he would say. "American soldier no good!"

Once I asked him what the Japs intended to do with all the prisoners they had taken in the islands. He laughed loudly, drew his sword and made a couple of decapitating motions with it.

He then asked me the value of various articles he had taken from American soldiers. While he was pulling them out I looked at one of his watches. It seemed familiar to me. When

I got a better view of it I saw that it was mine—an air forces watch with a twenty-four-hour dial I had bought on a flight to the island of Cebu. When he wanted to know how much it was worth I told him it cost only ten dollars.

119

I kept up the conversation, however, because I wanted some news from him, having had none in six weeks or so. When he realized what I wanted to know he was eager to tell me his version of it. He grinned and pulled out a map. He said: " Japanese soldiers win everywhere. Very brave."

I almost fainted when I looked at the map. It showed the entire Pacific theater. Japanese flags had been drawn on Java, Sumatra, New Guinea, Australia, the Hawaiians, and the Aleutians. Knowing the enemy had crushed us by sheer weight of numbers and equipment on Bataan, I thought it possible they had taken the other possessions.

I must have shown my consternation because the Jap now grinned more broadly than before. And he added: "That not all."

I wanted to know what else and was glad that I had. The answer dispelled all my doubts.

"Japanese submarines shell San Francisco," he said. "Japanese submarines shell Seattle. And, hah! Japanese submarines shell Chicago!"

I joined him in his laughter. It was the first real laugh I had had in what seemed like years. I was somewhat relieved.

When I returned to camp I found nearly everyone cheered up by the prospect of moving. Any place, we thought, would be better than O'Donnell. So we looked forward to Cabanatuan camp, which was to be our new home, according to the guards.

On the other hand the prospect worried us. A few weeks before, all the generals and full colonels had been removed to Japan and Formosa, where they were slaves in factories and on plantations. We knew our hope of exchange or escape would be nil if we were sent to either of these places. And the Cabanatuan story might be either a ruse to keep us quiet— or the Japanese conception of a joke.

But it turned out the reports were true. It was announced officially we were going to Cabanatuan, Nuevo Ecija, a camp for Americans only.

We were told that this time we were to ride in trucks, but that men who were unable to walk would have to be carried by the others to the north barricade of the prison. There we were to meet the trucks.

We spent all afternoon and the following night carrying men from our quarters to the loading place. We slept on the wet ground until time to start. Then we were lined up in the sun. There were no trucks. We were ordered to march.

Supporting those who were too weak to walk alone we straggled down the feeder road to the main highway. As we passed through the gates and into the hot highway I figured that we were on another death march and that we would lose about half our several hundred men.

Then the trucks came. They were Japanese army trucks, but they looked like home. There were Fords, Chevrolets, GMCs, and many others. The sight of them brought back memories of that terrible day when we left Bataan.

The Japs overloaded every one of them, packing prisoners in until there wasn't room to move. We didn't care, however. We were riding.

We probably wouldn't have been so cheerful if we had known what was in store for us at Cabanàtuan. After two and one-half hours of jolting and jogging we were there.

CHAPTER NINE

WHEN WE FIRST SAW the new prison camp we were overjoyed. It was far better than O'Donnell. As with O'Donnell, it had been built as a Filipino army camp, but it was a much better one and looked as though it had been completed.

On this trip the Jap guards lacked the venom the others had shown. The American-made trucks rolled us in through the western gate and along a road which ran between a Japanese army camp and hospital area on one side and the prison section on the other.

Our part of the camp was divided by barbed wire from the rest. There were large compounds; three for us with permanent wooden buildings and a fourth for Japanese recruits.

Along the east side were machine gun emplacements and three towers about forty feet high topped by guards, more machine guns, and the Japanese flag. Prisoners from Bataan and Corregidor already were there when we arrived.

They had named all roads and trails that connected the three compounds. There were Broadway, Market street, Michigan avenue, Main street, and many others.

A Milwaukee man had named a path for himself. It was Buboltz boulevard and led to the latrines.

Compounds No. 2 and No. 3 were upon high ground and well drained. Compound No. 1 was low and caught all the water that fell upon the high ground. The mud, we were to find, was knee deep. We were unloaded into compound No. 3.

As we piled out of the trucks that day I spotted some fellows I had known on Bataan. They had got to Corregidor and had been captured there. They didn't know me at first because of my ferocious looking beard, but they answered my wave.

We disposed of our sick. Then we mingled with the Corregidor boys and heard some good news. They had brought in razor blades. I found this out when I made myself known to four of them: Larry, Frankie, Bake, and Bill. Larry shaved off my beard and reported to the whole camp that he had found two Jap intelligence officers hiding in it with flare guns.

The first thing we thought about after getting shaved was, of course, eating. There had been no objection from the Jap guards about Larry's tonsorial activities.

Our first meal was of rice only. It was cleaner than that we had had at O'Donnell. As at O'Donnell, we had three meals a day; lugao (wet rice) for breakfast and drier rice for dinner and supper. After the first week there was green squash and a little of the juice from it.

Once a week each of us got a dried fish about four inches long and as thick as a man's finger; "dried stinkers," we called them. The Japs provided canned milk, one and one-half ounces a day for the sick men—at the start.

In the early days also, the men who went out on work details were given one hard bun to go with their rice. But as in the case of the milk the buns soon were discontinued.

The black market ran full blast. Jap soldiers bought food and other articles from Filipinos and smuggled them into the kitchens. There this stuff was parceled out to American soldiers and sailors on duty. The articles were peddled among the other prisoners at enormous profit to the Japs.

There was hardly an item—such as tinned fish, bar candy, or cigarettes—that didn't sell for five dollars. In the last days at Cabanatuan the Jap authorities established a sort of commissary in which most things that had sold formerly for five dollars were reduced to about forty cents. By that time, however, practically all our money had been spent in the black market. I had secreted my money—when I had it—inside my socks; between my toes to be exact. It was in fairly large bills and while it rubbed blisters and sometimes made walking painful, I held on to it.

The best eating at Cabanatuan was called "quan," a dish the prisoners developed. Quan is a Filipino word that has little meaning and can, therefore, be applied to almost anything. We used it to designate such extra food as we could get by fair means or otherwise.

We tried always to have among us some of the small tin buckets that were issued at the camp. These we called "quan" buckets. The recipe for "quan" follows:

Obtain from the black market or commissary a small can of fish and some coconut lard. At chow time get a mess kit filled with rice. After lining a "quan" bucket with lard, put in the rice along with some wild red peppers you have managed to gather while on jungle detail.

The bucket then goes into a bed of hot coals and the food

in it bakes. We thought it mighty fine, but if I never see any more of it, it will be all right with me.

This brings a memory of Lugao, of his short life and undeserved end. Lugao was a little white dog that wandered into Cabanatuan. He was just a handful of white fur and a bag of bones when he arrived. The boys on duty in the mess hall started feeding him on what rice and scraps they could spare. Dogs and cats in the Philippines eat rice, just as ours eat meat and drink milk.

Lugao [as has been said, the name means wet rice] began to fill out. Soon he was plump and sleek. Then, one day, he was missing.

Diligent inquiry eventually disclosed the facts. Lugao had wandered into a secluded spot where two sailors and a soldier were sitting thinking about how hungry they were. Lugao was "quanned."

Our food, however, was no more primitive than our method of eating it. There were no mess halls and we began taking the food to our barracks, but we gave up this practice. The rice drew flies which, like most undesirable mealtime guests, remained the rest of the day. So we took to squatting in the open to dine.

This started talk about the probability we wouldn't know how to act at splendid functions after the war. We wouldn't be able to balance teacups and salad plates on our knees or handle the table silver of civilization.

Furthermore, we wouldn't have read anything or have heard the latest songs. We probably would be busts at any gathering we might attend. So we worked out two surefire ways to distract attention from our awkwardness.

We decided that when food was served we would take our salads and teacups into a corner and eat like a pack of wolves. This would be taken by our hostess as (1) our peculiar whimsy or (2) would so startle her and the other guests that there would be no comment.

We agreed also that when anyone should approach and begin:

124

"My dear captain, have you read——" we would interrupt with:

"Now when I was on Bataan——."

It seemed to us that after this had happened four or five times in a single evening the words: "Now when I was on Bataan——" would be the signal for the hostess to whisper loudly: "For the love of Mike! Give the old fool a drink and shut him up!"

We liked this one so well that for a long time when you addressed a fellow prisoner he was quite likely to turn on you and yell: "Now when I was on Bataan——!" I think horseplay such as this did us more good than extra mess kits of rice.

The Jap guards, of course, thought we were deranged. Maybe we were. They were no less brutal than at O'Donnell, but they made this concession to officers: we were not required to go on labor details. Many did go because it seemed to us that the Japs pulled their punches somewhat when we were along.

These details of starved men were engaged in such work as wood chopping, path building, and barbed wire stringing. In addition they were sent out on heavy salvage work, picking up abandoned American and Japanese equipment on Bataan and in Manila. They helped build bridges and served as cargadores for the Jap troops hunting guerrilla forces in the hills.

It was not uncommon that twenty per cent of each detail would die on the job in a day or in the barracks that night. On one occasion nine men of a detail of twelve were left dead where they had fallen.

After seeing the type of work our soldiers and sailors were being required to do, I wondered that the casualties weren't one hundred per cent a day. The barbaric treatment that accompanied it was almost unbelievable.

Soon after our arrival the mass of incoming prisoners made it necessary that we move some wooden houses from the Jap military compound into our own. This operation was performed by running long poles beneath the structures, then lifting them to be carried across the road.

125

One Jap—a stocky, evil caricature on the human race—was armed with the shaft of a golf club. As the weakened men struggled to lift the building he ran up and down behind them, screaming like a maniac and beating them as though they were mules. Many fell under his blows, but that didn't end their beatings.

He is one Jap I'm going to catch if I have to chase him to Tokio. And I'm going to kill him, not with any weapon, but with the two hands God gave me.

[Editor's note—When this was written, Colonel Dyess had applied for reassignment to the Pacific theater.]

Some other Japs I hope to kill personally are those concerned in punishment inflicted upon some American soldiers who were caught accepting morsels of food slipped to them through the fence by kindly Filipino peasants, living near-by. These people took appalling risks to help us.

The soldiers involved were stripped of their shirts and flogged until their backs were raw. After the beating, an American doctor, also a prisoner, applied dresings. When he had ministered to the men and had gone, they were tied up again and flogged until the dressings were beaten into the open wounds.

This occurred in July, 1942. Up to this time I had escaped any major disaster, such as serious illness. I had taken my beatings and kickings along with the rest and had hoped I would keep my health. But my turn was just around the corner.

Through the steaming and filthy camp that month, there swept a series of epidemics that took an appalling toll of lives.

Sanitary conditions at Cabanatuan, while better than those at O'Donnell, were, nevertheless, terrible. The latrines were long, open ditches that filled the area with an ever present stench and bred millions of flies and mosquitoes. Bathing and laundry work were done in muddy sinkholes.

I lived now with twelve other fellows in a building in the lowlands, having been transferred from the higher ground of the camp. Our room, about sixteen by eighteen feet, was filthy because we had no way of cleaning it. We all slept on the floor.

I first fell victim to yellow jaundice, which was present in epidemic form. Diphtheria also was prevalent, but I escaped that. Next a dengue mosquito got me, so I had jaundice and dengue fever at the same time.

My first intimation that I really was sick came during a game of soft ball one Sunday afternoon. You may think it was idiotic of men in our condition to play athletic games, but our desire for something like normal recreation was almost as strong as our physical hunger. We felt that anything approximating the social gatherings and routine of the world outside would ease our minds.

After we had been at Cabanatuan two weeks, the Japs yielded to the entreaties of our Protestant and Catholic chaplains that we have Sunday services. This accomplished, the chaplains began suggesting recreation of some sort. One of them had a happy thought and intimated we might work better if given a little time to play. The Japs seized upon that. We were allowed to hold an amateur variety show once a week, for the entertainment of ourselves and the Jap soldiers.

We had a guitar and trumpet, complete with players, and some good singers. We all joined in on the old songs—"Let Me Call You Sweetheart," "My Old Kentucky Home," "There's a Long, Long Trail," and others. Military and patriotic songs were barred. We did skits that burlesqued one another. We would have dearly loved to present a couple putting Hirohito and Tojo on the pan, but there were too many Jap guards around the low platform on which we staged the shows.

Though they could understand little of what went on, the Japs appeared to enjoy our entertainments and in a burst of generosity announced we might play American baseball. They even came up with a soft ball.

We carved bats of native wood and laid out a diamond on the inspection ground. Before long, however, we found we were overtaxing ourselves and building monumental appetites so we slowed down considerably. I remember thinking as I watched the play one day that it was like a slow-motion film of a normal game.

The game that caused my ailments to flare up was played on an extremely hot afternoon. I had knocked a ball past shortstop and was hotfooting it for first base, when I felt suddenly as if I were passing out. I got on the ground as quickly as possible. When the dizziness passed I tried to walk back to the bench. Another wave hit me and I went down again. One of the fellows helped me totter over to the barracks.

I turned the color of lemon rind and was unable to eat. Growing rapidly weaker, I realized I'd have to force myself to retain some food. But day after day as I approached the stench of the kitchens I would have to turn back.

I felt that if I could get some milk, eggs, or Albany [Tex.] fried chicken I'd be all right. Then it seemed that dreams were about to come true. The Jap guards announced chicken and eggs were to be served to the prisoners. They were.

There were three chickens to be divided among five hundred men. There were eighteen eggs for the same group. But we never saw any more chicken or any more eggs.

[Editor's note—Shortly after this the Tokio propaganda radio announced that American prisoners in the Philippines were being fed on chicken and eggs.]

I don't want to seem to be dwelling upon my sufferings. I do it simply because mine were typical of the diseases that racked many another American soldier. And most of the others probably are not alive today.

Some of the boys in our room set out to forage for me when it seemed my sickness was taking that turn we all knew so well. All of us were out of money, having spent it in the black market maintained by Jap soldiers. The commissary recently established by Jap authorities therefore was closed to us.

Captain Burt—whose full name I wish I could tell—managed somehow, somewhere, to get money and to buy a can of American yellow clingstone peaches and a can of fish. A kid we called Potee succeeded in snaking some sugar out of the kitchen. These things saved me.

The Japs would do nothing except tell me to go to the hospital. That, I was determined not to do, knowing that those who entered that disease-ridden sty rarely came out alive.

The hospital was a place without beds, the men lying on raised bamboo shelves. There was a primitive operating room that almost never was in operation and a dispensary that seldom dispensed anything.

When a man neared death from dysentery, malaria, wet or dry beriberi, diphtheria, or any one of the other plagues that were sweeping the place, he was removed to another building which we called St. Peter's ward. And there he died.

The death rate at Cabanatuan prison in July was thirty Americans a day. It went up steadily. In the first few months, the Japs contended there were no medicines for anyone, not even themselves.

Later in the summer they permitted the International Red Cross in Manila to ship in some medicines, but these they left in the packing cases for weeks, while hundreds of men died. We knew the medicines were there, because we had unloaded them from trucks and had read the labels.

The shipment included serum which would have saved many diphtheria victims, quinine which would have cut to a minimum the malaria deaths, dressings and antiseptics for the wounds the Japs inflicted daily, and precious, nourishing products that would have enabled the patients to fight beriberi and blindness that resulted from lack of vitamins. The last cases were the most heartrending of all.

Every man values his sight. Knowing what an airplane pilot's sight means to him, it almost destroyed me to see some of them groping their way around the stinking prison of Cabanatuan.

One of these men insisted that something be done for him. And for once the Jap operating room operated. The pilot was relieved of one of his blind eyes.

When I recovered what passed for health in Cabanatuan—

after six weeks of being flat on my back—my weight was 120 pounds. Normally it is around 175. But even at 120 I was considered a fat man—so skinny were the others. When I left the camp on October 26, 1942, there were 2,500 Americans sick in their barracks, in the hospital, or in St. Peter's ward. I doubt that any of them recovered.

The basic reason for these deaths was malnutrition. It was proved by autopsies performed both by American and Japanese doctors. When it had been established, beyond doubt, that the men were starving to death, the Japs were forced to admit it. Their answer was that they were sorry; the circumstance was regrettable: there simply was no food. Yet the islands—all of them—had an abundance of food, as we all knew.

I could talk all year about conditions at Cabanatuan. I could tell about our futile rage at the daily sight of the Stars and Stripes being used as a scrub rag, pot wiper, and floor mop in the reeking Japanese kitchens. Sometimes the flag was used to wrap up scraps and remnants. It was even kicked around underfoot.

United protests by officers and men brought blank silences or sneers. One day the flag disappeared. We heard a Japanese officer had ordered its removal from the kitchen. But I like to believe that some American succeeded in rescuing and destroying it in the manner officially designated; by burning.

In general it may be said that our physical surroundings were better that those at O'Donnell. We got more food and our living quarters were somewhat better. But Cabanatuan far excelled the first camp in sadistic cruelty and barbaric punishments.

Early in our stay a middle-aged colonel, adjutant of American headquarters—a co-ordinating agency set up for assembling work details and keeping count of us—was a victim of uncalled-for brutality. He had personally delivered to Japanese headquarters one of the complicated forms that had to be filled out daily. There was a slight error and the Jap adjutant went into a rage. The Jap interpreter grew even more infuriated than his superior. He shouted that all Americans are sons of dogs. The colonel turned to leave the room. The interpreter sprang after him and beat him insensible with a blackjack.

During the remainder of my stay there the American officer was a victim of violent headaches. They would prostrate him forty-eight hours at a time. He was stricken at least twice a week.

Soon after our arrival the Japs set out to impress us with the futility of attempting to escape. They advised that we organize an inner wall patrol to save our own men from the consequences of rash efforts to get away. Every two or three days we were summoned to attend a spectacle that was sort of a ghastly parody on the old-time American medicine show. It will be recalled that some of the nomadic medicine men used to exhibit deformed or afflicted human freaks to attract a crowd.

The Jap counterpart of the medicine man was a noncommissioned officer who stood on a platform to address us. With him were his freaks: two American naval officers who had gotten away, but had been forced by hunger to give themselves up. They had been put on a rice and water diet and set at hard labor. They were like living skeletons and grew thinner and weaker at each appearance. Sometimes the Jap also exhibited an American soldier, an Indian, who also had escaped only to surrender. His feet were hobbled, his arms tied, and he was led around by a halter fastened about his neck. On his chest was a sign that read: "I tried to escape." The medicine man's speech always was the same:

"It is ver' bad to try escape. You not should try. Conditions soon big better here. We do everything to make better. You not should escape." He then would point to his miserable trio and say:

"These are three that try escape. You see, they come back to us. You see what is becoming of them. You not should try escape."

There came a day when the navy officers were seen no longer. They had not escaped again. We'd have known about that. They just were no longer there. A few days later the

131

hobbled and placarded Indian was gone. There was only one medicine show after that. The Jap noncom, deprived of his cast, seemed to have lost his stage presence.

The first murders at Cabanatuan—the first I witnessed, that is—came soon afterward. They involved five American soldiers and a Filipino civilian. The six were engaged in a black market enterprise. The Filipino obtained the articles of sale— items of food, razor blades, soap, and so on, and slipped them through the fence at night to the Americans. The prices were much more reasonable than those in the black market operated by the Jap inner guards, who were determined to break up the rival ring. They watched the compounds and the fences many nights before they were successful. It never was established whether the Filipino bribed the Jap outer guards or whether he knew their movements well enough to elude them. When the inner guards finally scored, however, they caught everyone concerned; the Filipino and all five Americans. The prisoners were kept under guard all night.

At sunrise they were stripped of their clothing, tied up in the glaring sunlight and flogged. When the sun was directly overhead, the six were flogged again.

During the afternoon one of the soldiers became delirious and broke his bonds. He ran to the barracks, drank all the water he could find, and lay down on his mat. The Japs were after him in a few minutes. They dragged him back to the whipping post, trussed him up, and flogged all six of the prisoners again. Meanwhile, several men had been detailed to dig a shallow trench a short distance from camp. At sundown the sufferers were freed of their ropes and were marched naked to the trench where a firing squad shot them to death.

It was the frequent recurrence of such tortures and wanton murder at Cabanatuan that led eventually to one of the most terrible spectacles I ever have witnessed.

Two lieutenant colonels of the United States army and a navy lieutenant determined they would escape if they died in the attempt. They were so desperate that they made their effort in daylight, practically under the eyes of guards on towers that overlooked the camp and of Japs waiting behind machine gun emplacements just outside the barbed wire barricade.

The American officers planned to crawl on their bellies down a drainage ditch to a small opening beneath the barricade. The jungle was the only place to which they could have gone. Without supplies and equipment there, their chances would have been just about nil. And before reaching the jungle they would have had to elude the Jap walking patrol, which supplemented the tower and machine gun guards.

They started inching their way through the filthy ditch that reeked of human waste. The noon sun blazed down on them. They had taken nothing with them—no water, food, or maps. They were weaponless, though weapons would have done them no good. As they were nearing the fence someone caused a noise and the Jap patrol heard it.

In a second or two there was a hullabaloo of shrieking and chattering from the runts outside the fence. Japs ran from all directions toward the ditch. The three American officers were hauled out. This was the first the rest of us prisoners knew of what was happening.

When I saw the three standing under guard before a Jap officer, I had a sinking feeling. I thought I knew what was coming, but I never could have imagined the things that now took place.

The ragged, faded, and torn uniforms were stripped off the prisoners by their guards. The naked men then were marched through the glare of the steaming prison camp. Near the front, or western gate, they were flogged almost into insensibility.

Bleeding and dazed, they were led outside. Their hands were tied behind them. Additional ropes were brought and these were tied to the fastened hands and secured to cross pieces some feet above the victims' heads. This forced them to stand always erect, almost on tiptoes. Slumping possibly would have dislocated the arms at the shoulders. The posture was agonizing.

133

A short two-by-four timber was placed near-by. As Filipinos approached on the road, the Jap guards, their eyes glittering, forced the passersby to pick up the timber and smash each of the three American officers in the face. The first few blows broke their noses.

As the men revived slightly from each clubbing, Jap guards laid on with whips. Every blow could be heard down in our barracks. Every blow brought a flow of blood. The burning sun rays dried the blood in black clots. It stuck to the officers' legs and backs like tar.

This all was taking place in view of the other prisoners. We could hear the crunchy sound as the timber, swung by unwilling Filipinos, crashed into the faces—now almost unrecognizable. Again and again, between blows, would come the slither and slash of the whips.

Seeing this go on, hour after hour, put into me a feeling I cannot define. I can try only to describe it. It was not hatred, as such. I had been hating the Japs for months. I had taken pleasure in killing them on Bataan; pleasure derived from the memories of what they had done to Clark and Nichols fields and to my friends on the first day of the war.

I had come to hate the Japs through every waking hour and to dream my hatred when I slept. This feeling now was a a combination of cold disgust such as you have for a rattlesnake and a physical sympathetic suffering for those three victims.

Night came and they still were there. The sun went down. Lights were visible out by the gate. And, intermittently, we could hear, above the noises of the camp, the sound of the whip.

I think I prayed that night that those men could die soon. I had no hope that they would survive. Yet, when morning came—after I had had an hour or so of tormented sleep—they still were there.

This day passed as had the first. By its end there was no conversation in camp. No one spoke. We watched these men in their Gethsemane and could find no words. After another night, in which I had practically no sleep, it began again.

There were the floggings and the blows in the face with the two-by-fours. Everyone who came down that road of horror had to take his turn at slamming the blood-soaked timber into the smashed faces.

What held them up, I don't know. There are men who can die easily, if they decide to give up the struggle. Yet you'd be surprised how hard it is to pound or torture the life spark out of a man who has willed to live.

In these two lieutenant colonels and the naval lieutenant, the Japs seemed to have found three who were determined to live. They would not give up. On the third day a typhoon swept in.

During the afternoon the three victims stood naked and shivering in the downpour. The rain cleansed their wounds and bodies at times, but the Japs opened new wounds with the whip as often as they thought they could do so without killing.

At length the rain ceased. There now was little hope on the part of the Jap officers that the men could survive longer. There were commands and a stir among Jap noncommissioned officers. We stood wet and bedraggled, watching through the barbed wire.

In the last flogging, a slash of the keen, hissing whip had severed one colonel's ear, except for a strip of flesh that kept it attached. The ear now hung down on his shoulder.

From a building a squad of Japanese soldiers emerged. A noncommissioned officer carried an armload of rifles. A covered truck pulled up. The rifles were put in, followed by the men.

From another direction a file of Jap soldiers carrying shovels made their appearance. They also entered the truck, each with his shovel. At the command of Jap commissioned officers, the bonds of the American officers were cut and the three were thrown into the truck.

One of the Jap officers, wearing a heavy sword, seated himself beside the driver. The motor was started and they rolled away, under a lowering sky. We heard the machine stop just out of sight of camp.

There was a wait, a volley, then another. We didn't understand why the squad had fired only twice.

Eventually the truck rolled back and stopped. The soldiers got out and our guards talked to them. Then the guards came over to the barbed wire barricade, yapping, bobbing their heads, and gesturing. They told us what had happened.

One colonel and the naval officer had been shot. The Jap officer had done the other colonel of the United States army "the honor of beheading him personally." The three had been buried at the scene of their deaths.

We slept that night, from sheer exhaustion, I think. There were not many words exchanged in camp for several days. And we hardly looked at our guards, but when something particularly unpleasant was brewing we usually could sense it from their conduct.

There is one morning in September, 1942, that I'll never forget. Our keepers were angrier and grimmer than I'd ever seen them.

News spread that a Jap soldier, one of the guards, had been killed, presumably by a Filipino, the head of a barrio [hamlet], a mile or so on the road from Cabanatuan. Our only sorrow at these tidings was that one of ourselves had not done it.

About 11 A.M., we saw machine gun and mortar units moving away from Jap military headquarters. They passed through the gates and disappeared in the direction of the barrio. At noon we heard them firing and saw long plumes of smoke rising.

A little later a procession of pro-Jap Filipinos moved down the road, their arms filled with loot from the burning houses. Why the Japs let anyone else have any loot always has been a mystery to me. We learned that all inhabitants of the barrio had been wiped out by shellfire and flames. These numbered forty or fifty men, women, and babies.

At the head of the procession, on horseback, was the Jap officer who had led the expedition of two hundred soldiers. Behind him marched two soldiers carrying a pole upon which was stuck the head of a Filipino.

This grisly souvenir was paraded through the camp, then was set up outside the main gate. Beneath the head was an inscription in English and Japanese: "A Very Bad Man."

CHAPTER TEN

IN OCTOBER, 1942, MY DAYS at Cabanatuan were coming to an end. And, I thought, so was I. But before my days ended there I was able to pick up some knowledge of the Japs that should be of great value to me when I face them in battle again. It may prove helpful to others of our fighting men who may read this.

It concerns the Japs' national inferiority complex and their methods of training soldiers for battle. The observations that follow come partially from experience and partially from study and inquiry inspired by experience. It has long been a military maxim that an understanding of your enemy's thought processes is a powerful weapon against him.

The event that crystallized a number of my half-formed theories and led to my efforts at understanding the Jap occurred one morning when several American officers were sitting and lounging about on the bamboo floor of our barracks room. A Jap three-star private entered. We all jumped up, snapped to attention, and saluted. He acknowledged the salutes with a grunt and started looting our packs.

Suddenly the Jap uttered an angry yell and held up a watch he had found in one of them. He walked over and stared at us fixedly in turn. I was the tallest man there.

He hopped over and walloped me in the face, first with his right, then with his left hand. He stood roughly five feet, his head coming about to my breastbone, but he was stocky and strong. By the time he had socked me twenty times or so, I was practically down to his size. It would have been suicide to resist. He took a final punch and walked out.

We sat around and talked awhile. The others suggested the little so-and-so be knocked off and the body dropped into a latrine. Knowing how the Japs felt about us, however, we figured they knew pretty well how we felt about them. If one of their soldiers should turn up missing they'd look in the latrine.

The result would be the visitation of some terrible punishment upon all the prisoners in camp. But that is beside the point.

The little slugger's choice of the tallest man present for his abuse—knowing he would be backed up by Jap authority—illustrates the Jap inferiority complex. The Jap always feels inferior in the presence of the American. If for no other reason, it is because Americans are white, are taller, usually, and better looking.

We learned never to look a Jap in the eye—even the lowest, one-star private. No Jap inferior may look a superior in the eye. They were quick to club us down and kick us when we forgot we were captives and not honorable prisoners of war.

The Japanese are a nation of houseboys. The treatment they may expect from their superiors does little to lift them from their low mental state. This is particularly true in the Jap army. It has been said the Jap army is the best-disciplined body of men in the world. There is rigid discipline there, but it is one of fear. The Jap soldier fears his own officers far more than he does the enemy.

Jap soldiers must submit to beatings with the fist or sluggings with the gun butt when they diplease a superior officer. Two-star privates are privileged to beat one-star privates. A commissioned officer can be a courtmartial and executioner—and at two seconds' notice.

At Cabanatuan we had ample opportunity to watch the training and development of the Japanese soldier. The recruits came in in bunches and were quartered and drilled in the compound just south of our own.

A year is required for a recruit to rise to the rank of private. During his first six months he wears a patched, cast-off uniform bearing a triangular, numbered tag which is sewed on his blouse over the left pocket. At the end of the first period he gets an oblong patch, bearing one bar if he has been a fair to middling pupil and two if he has done excellently. At the end of a year the patch is replaced by a star and he is a private. The soldier's first promotion gives him an additional star and his next adds a third.

After one of the early skirmishes near Manila, it was reported by some American troops who didn't understand the three-star rating system that they had just killed fifty-three Japanese generals! Three-star privates rate about as corporals do in our army, and we were warned to steer clear of them. The lowest noncommissioned officer wears one star with a horizontal bar through it. His rank is comparable to that of an American sergeant.

Noncommissioned officers are permitted only to slug or beat the men serving under them. The right of summary execution with pistol or by beheadal is reserved to the commissioned officers.

There is a popular misconception, which seems to have become prevalent during the Russo-Japanese war of 1904, that the Japanese soldier lives on a handful of rice and a dried fish a day. Nothing could be farther from the truth. I have seen what they eat under war conditions. They put away beef, pork, chicken or lamb, high protein soybean sauce, greens, potatoes, fish, fruits and high potency vitamin tablets. They are bowlegged and funny looking but they are powerful physically.

The recruits at Cabanatuan came mostly from Formosa. After they had been on army rations a few days we could almost see them begin to grow and put on flesh and brawn. All day long they would march up and down, goose-stepping, and practicing with the bayonet, to the accompaniment of their weird marching chants, which they howled at the tops of their voices.

The bayonet practice put us into stitches, those of us who

were strong enough to laugh, that is. They have but one bayonet stroke, a long, lunging thrust. The face sometimes is averted after the thrust has been aimed at the subject. The stroke usually is accompanied by a fiendish yell that sounds like "Yaaaaaah!" Apparently the Jap soldier is taught nothing about the butt stroke or the parrying stroke.

When an American soldier charges he holds his rifle across his body obliquely, stock down and in the right hand. The barrel is gripped by the left.

When he is ready to fall prone, to a firing position, the American soldier drops to one knee, brings the rifle stock down upon the ground to break his fall, and goes over on his stomach ready to open fire.

The Japanese rifle will not take this kind of treatment. The Jap, of necessity, charges with the gun at his side in the right hand. He gets to the ground as best he can. Often he simply goes down, losing his rifle as he sprawls. There is a wild scramble to recover it and start shooting.

Our next best laughs came from watching the bowlegged Japs as they tried the goose step. The spectacle, as I recall it, justifies use of an archaic literary expression; it beggared description. The Jap soldier is a funny little man. But make no mistake; he is as deadly as a cobra.

His real vulnerability lies in his fear of losing face. This also is a national trait and is true of all Japs, civil or military, high or low. The Jap, more than any other national, is concerned by what others think of him. When a majority looks down upon him or disapproves of his actions he is said to have lost face. He will either change his ways, try to justify them, or commit hari kiri, depending upon the seriousness of the reproach.

This is one of the reasons why I believe disclosure of Japanese cruelty and starvation in the prison camps will redound to the benefit of the American and Filipino prisoners who may still be alive there. The entire civilized world will look in disgust upon Japan when the truth is known. And I feel that in this case, the Japanese will change their ways.

This belief was shared by my comrades at O'Donnell, Cabanatuan, and Davao. Their consuming desire was that the people at home know, in full and stark detail, the barbaric punishments inflicted upon them by their captors. Once when we discussed the possibility of the truth some day coming out, someone suggested it might result in rougher treatment from the Japs. But our feeling always was that the Japs had done everything to us they could; that if they did devise new horrors we would be willing to take them in the knowledge the American people had been apprised of the truth and would one day exact a terrible revenge.

There was practically nothing we could do in that direction; we could not take physical revenge upon our tormentors, but there were many ways we could, and did, outwit them. There were many things they were itching to find out about the American army and it strengthened our morale every time we were able to give them the runaround.

There was an occasion during the last days at Cabanatuan that will linger in my memory always. It left an unforgettably pleasant afterglow. I felt as I had the day I shot down my first Jap plane.

It began one fall morning before dawn when I was routed out of bed along with two other officers and three sergeants. We were piled into a Japanese army truck—a Ford, incidentally—surrounded by guards. As we rolled through the gates a Buick, filled with Jap officers, took its place behind us. We were told only that we were bound for military headquarters in Manila.

The friendliness and compassion of the Filipino people has been mentioned before, but on the trip into the city and while there we had additional and comforting evidences of it. We had covered about thirty-five of the seventy-five miles when our truck broke down. When we piled out we saw we were in front of a bamboo food stand.

The smell of cooking was too much for me. I asked a Jap commissioned officer if we would be permitted to buy a little something at the stand. He looked at me in amazement.

"You mean you hungry?" he asked, raising his brows.

Did I mean we were hungry! All six of us wouldn't have

tipped the beam at five hundred pounds. I reminded him we had eaten nothing that day. The Jap pondered this a full minute. Then he jerked his head toward the stand. "Go!" he said.

We went. The Filipinos gave us four times the amount of food we paid for. There were plates of soft, boiled corn; boiled eggs, rice balls, greens, and fruit. It was the first real meal we had had since the fall of Bataan. We were new men when we climbed back aboard.

We were anxious to see what effect the war was having on Manila. When we rolled in we could see little change, except that the streets were pretty well deserted both of vehicular and pedestrian traffic. We saw almost no evidence of bomb and fire damage. The Filipinos made secret signs of friendship and encouragement. I saw one man looking at us intently.

He was holding a cigarette in the crotch of his first and second fingers, which formed a V for Victory. Another had thrust his thumb inside his belt. The downthrust fingers formed a V. We saw many Vs as we rolled through the streets.

As we pushed in toward the heart of the city, vendors began tossing sweets into the truck. One man raced along beside us tossing in his entire, scanty stock. Then he fled down an alley, abandoning the cart. The guards glared, but did not pursue. Nor did they interfere as we ate our windfall of popsicles, ice cream bars, and candy. This was strange behavior indeed. We got the idea the Japs wanted something from us and had ordered we be humored to some extent. And so it turned out.

Our truck stopped on Taft avenue, and we were taken into a building where we were shown photographs of our air warning equipment. They were old sets and some had been damaged by explosions. The Japs wanted to know if we knew what they were. We scratched our heads.

A sergeant said he thought one looked like a radio set. I said I thought they looked like some new type radio transmitter. These questions told us what we wanted to know. We were forewarned. Our next stop was a Manila hotel and we paraded our rags and dirt through the splendid lobby.

We were escorted to a suite where we were greeted by high Japanese officers. They seated us in easy chairs and ordered ice water for us. Ice water! It was something to dream about.

And all the time they treated us as honored guests. There were even cigarettes. Then the questioning began. Could we tell them something of our most efficient air warning service? Where were the sets located? We told them, of course, that these matters were kept secret even from officers and that we knew nothing.

As the questioning went on, it became obvious the Japs wanted the answer to a specific problem that had been bothering them. Presently it came out. They recalled that their planes had caught us unaware at Pearl Harbor. Considering our excellent air warning service, how had this happened?

"I never was at Pearl Harbor," I said. "I don't know what happened."

"But," said one officer, "we caught the American planes on the ground at Clark field, here. How did that happen?"

"I wasn't at Clark field until later. I was at Nichols field when you caught them." It all connected up in my mind now. They were trying to find out if the direction and altitude of a bomber's approach made a difference in our sets. This was proved the next instant.

Pressing more ice water and cigarettes upon us, one of the officers leaned forward and, in a confidential tone, asked:

"Would it be better that our planes fly very low or very high?"

I realized I was wearing out our welcome, but I told him I never had been told anything about the air warning service; that I was just a dumb Texas boy, so would not have caught on if I had been told.

This put a distinct chill into the air, though it was a hot day. A Jap civilian, who I later learned only recently had arrived from Washington—and I still wonder how he got there—began to get to the root of the matter in a very businesslike way.

There undoubtedly were certain men in the United States army who knew about air raid warning equipment? I had to answer that in the affirmative. And there were also schools, no doubt? I had to acknowledge that also. And now came the sixty-four dollar question:

"Name and locate these schools!"

I told him I knew of only one. Then I named a little place where I knew there wasn't any such thing. The Japs thought they had got their information. Their courtesy vanished and we were dismissed with grunts.

The guards returned us to our trucks, which took us to Manila's Old Bilibid prison. There we stayed until we were returned to camp. Just before we left, however, there were hints that anyone who wanted to be a camp stool pigeon for the Imperial Japanese army would do well. But offers like this were old stuff.

We heard one other thing that was interesting: the Jap army air force hadn't had the nerve to tackle Pearl Harbor and had insisted the raid could not be carried off; that they all would be shot down, the strategy of the Japs would be exposed without striking an effective blow, and that Japanese everywhere would lose face.

Opportunists in the Jap navy took the other view. Their air force, they said, could carry it off. So the stab in the back attack on Pearl Harbor was a Jap navy show. The army air force had no part in it.

But the thing that made all us prisoners walk out of there like new men was the knowledge the Japs knew nothing of our air warning service, or anything connected with it. And we had outwitted them. It was a grand feeling.

And another treat was in store for me. A little later—back at Cabanatuan—I was summoned to Jap headquarters along with five lieutenant colonels who had served in air force headquarters on Bataan. We were questioned by two Jap pilots whose rank would correspond with that of an American first lieutenant.

The same old, oily courtesy prevailed and we were given glasses of warm milk, bowls of tea, ice water, and American cigarettes. But things quickly took a dangerous turn. They wanted to know the armament carried by a P-40 pursuit plane. Knowing that the Japs had examined P-40 wrecks on Bataan, I told him the truth: Six .50-caliber machine guns.

The Jap who had assumed the lead in questioning us was sitting, curling and wiggling his bare toes. Now he leaped from his chair, dancing, gesticulating and yelling:

"Lie! Lie! Not machine guns; cannon!" The group of guards near-by came to alert immediately. I tried to explain through the interpreter that though the Japs might call them cannon, we called them machine guns.

One of the colonels told me quickly in a low voice to translate the guns' caliber into millimeters. This I did, and the Japs readily saw that though there was quite a difference between his .27-caliber gun and our .50-caliber, we simply called ours machine guns because they were automatic fire.

"Oh! Okay," he said and resumed his seat, wiggling his toes. Then came the scene I wouldn't mind reliving every day. The Jap wanted to know what I had done in the war and I told him I had done very little; that I had had little chance to fly, as I was one of the inferior pilots.

"Don't be 'fraid," he said. "Tell what you done." Then, using the interpreter, he told me this: "Fear nothing. If you have shot down Japanese airplanes it is a thing to be proud of."

I was a sap to do it, but the little Jap had appeared so cocky and proud of himself that I thought I would just hang a few on him. I told him that I had shot a Japanese plane.

"What happen?" he asked quickly.

I made an upward gesture with both hands and yelled: "BOOOM!"

"Oooooo!" he moaned and sat a long time looking at his toes, which now had ceased wiggling. I think that for the first time I saw a Jap register sorrow. Eventually, he looked up again.

"You shoot more than one Japanese plane? Two? Three? Don't be 'fraid."

I told him that I had shot more than one.

"How many? What happen?" he asked.

So I let him have it with gestures.

"BOOM! BOOM! BOOM! BOOM! BOOM! BOOM! BOOM! BOOM!"

With the last "boom" I realized I probably was the biggest sap who ever wore an American uniform. I figured the guards behind me even now were getting ready to go into action. Nothing happened, however, except that the little pilot gave the weirdest and most dismal groan I ever have heard and sat with hands clasped, rocking to and fro in his chair.

There was a long and uncomfortable silence during which I sat wondering what I had in my head, brains or marbles. At length the little Jap looked up, gave a few preliminary wiggles of the toes, and began again. He wanted to know the names of the pilots who had shot down certain planes near our airports during the fighting on Bataan. I remembered some of them and gave him names of pilots I knew to be dead or who had escaped to Australia before the surrender.

He asked about the pilot who in late March had downed a plane flown by a Japanese commissioned officer near our present prison camp. I remembered the fight well. Lieutenant Stone had done a neat bit of flying and shooting on that occasion. The Jap pilot had been both brave and clever. Since Stone was out of reach of the Japs I gave his name. The little pilot shook his head dolefully.

"This Lieutenant Stone he kill my squadron leader," he said in a voice so somber it was almost as though he expected me to commiserate with him.

It crossed my mind to say: "Tst, tst, tst. Lieutenant Stone was a bad boy. Always killing Japs. Why, you know, that boy killed every Jap he saw." But this time I had sense enough to keep my big mouth shut. I next was asked about the relative speeds of our planes.

"P-40. We hear it go 660 kilometers (400 miles) per hour. True, or propaganda?"

"Propaganda," I said. "Only about 580 kilometers (350 miles) an hour."

146

"Hah! P-38. We hear it go 750 kilometers per hour. True or propaganda?"

"Not true and not propaganda," I said. "P-38 goes 830 kilometers (500 miles) an hour."

"Oh! Oh! Oh! . . . No!"

"Yes. True."

"Oooooooh!" Another silence, accompanied by vigorous toe wiggling. Then he asked suddenly:

"You see No. 1 Japanese plane?"

I said I hadn't. Then he described it and I realized I had. One come over the Mariveles mountain one day in March as I was returning from a mission. The Jap saw me and banked away, heading westward. He left me as though I were nailed down.

"Japanese No. 1 plane fastest in world," continued the pilot. "We have races at Tokio and No. 1 plane beat Messerschmitt 110 and beat best Italian plane." I didn't doubt it. "Japanese all over world send money to build No. 1 plane. Soon we have many." I said nothing.

The little Jap ended the conversation abruptly by putting on his shoes. He seemed very thoughtful as he prepared to take his leave. My replies, I realized, had not made the Jap air force appear any too good. At the door he turned back.

"Before war; you know Japanese planes fly over Philippines every night without interfered with?"

I said I had known it. He slapped his short legs and howled with laughter. He had saved face both for the Jap air force and himself. He controlled himself long enough to add: "You see me soon again; very soon." He still was laughing like a hyena when he entered the car in front of headquarters. I didn't like that last crack, but I walked down the hill greatly heartened. Not only had we hoodwinked the Japs again, but I actually had caused one of them a little grief. Even the filthy rice tasted good that night.

About half an hour later two planes roared across the camp so low our shacks trembled and vibrated. It was my little friend and his partner homeward bound with a load of mis-

147

information. I was greatly relieved. I knew then what he had meant by his closing remark. I seemed to have implanted in him a little respect for the Americans. I think he wanted to show me that he, too, could fly an airplane.

CHAPTER ELEVEN

LATE IN OCTOBER, 1942, things were astir in Cabanatuan prison. Not long before then, the Japs had searched out four hundred men with technical knowledge, had given them physical examinations and new clothing, and had put them aboard a ship bound for Japan, where they were to be factory slaves.

Now the same thing was starting again. They were looking for a thousand men this time. We were told, however, that no one need go if he could find someone to take his place. There were rumors, too, that the one thousand were bound, not for Japan, but for Davao prison colony on Mindanao island.

I didn't want to go to Japan, where there would be no chance of escape, but I was so sick of Cabanatuan I would have been willing to go almost anywhere. So I got out a deck of greasy cards and dealt two poker hands. The north hand represented Cabanatuan and the south Mindanao. North lost to a pair of aces, so I announced I was ready to pack up.

On October 24, we were lined up and divided into companies of two hundred men each. There were sick men in the lines and thirty-one of these were pulled out and left behind for such treatment as Cabanatuan offered.

The rest of us were marched the four miles into the town of Cabanatuan and loaded into narrow gauge boxcars. For a change, the Japs left the doors open, and we had ventilation.

We reached Manila that afternoon, were held in the cars until night, then were marched through the deserted streets to Old Bilibid prison. There we slept on concrete floors, but it wasn't so bad, because the Japs fed us mutton soup and rice on our arrival.

The next day, October 25, we were assembled in companies and started off down the street. We realized at once that this was another victory march such as the Corregidor prisoners made, one of those marches so dear to the Japanese heart.

We marched through the maze of Manila streets for a long time. Several of the Jap leaders became separated from the main company and took their men up and down and around and about for hours. The search for these groups prolonged the march of the others.

The Filipinos who lined the streets looked at us silently and with compassion. The women wept openly. Wherever we looked, people covertly were making the V for victory sign. From the Jap point of view, the march was a flop. The attitude of the populace discouraged even the Jap soldiers who stood here and there along the streets; soldiers such as those who cursed and abused the Corregidor prisoners.

We arrived at the docks in late evening. Before us lay our ship, a 7,000-ton British-built vessel which had been refitted first as a Japanese troopship and later as a combination cargo and convict ship.

I think it must have been the filthiest vessel ever to put to sea. The deck was heaped with goods and junk of all kinds.

The hold in which we were to sleep smelled almost as bad as the hospitals at O'Donnell and Cabanatuan prison camps.

Areas had been boxed off throughout the hold, and twelve men were assigned to each. There was room for only six to sleep at one time. The Jap troops had left millions of lice and bedbugs. In a few hours we were crawling with them.

Beneath the below-decks section where we were assigned the Japs had stored a large quantity of gasoline. This added to the medley of smells. I took all this in, then went back on

149

deck, to get away from the stifling heat and to find out where we were going.

The blacked-out ship eased away from the dock and slid out into the shadows of Manila bay. A rising breeze carried off some of the reek that rose from the vile regions below. The gasoline fumes had seemed to lend carrying power to the smells, permeating the entire area, before the start. The fresh, tangy air of the bay was a blessed relief.

It was impossible, of course, to see the opposite shore, twenty-five miles or so away in the darkness to the west. I was not unmindful of it, however. Along there just six months before we had staggered on in the Death March from Bataan. How many of my old comrades lay in shallow graves beside that route, murdered by the buzzard squad? There will never be any way of telling. We had been informed the Japs often removed and destroyed identification tags of the men they murdered, so that their bodies might never be claimed and honored. I saw it happen once—when the delirious and comatose men were buried alive during the Death March.

I tried without success to rid myself of these dismal thoughts as our ship sloshed and rolled down the bay. I was dog tired but I felt I couldn't sleep until I knew whether our destination was to be Mindanao or Japan. I must have dozed a while. The next I remember is straining my eyes through the starlit night at the dark and silent bulk of Corregidor, off to the right.

As I stared, the rocky mass seemed to be moving; slipping around to get behind us. Suddenly I knew we were changing our course, heading due south. This meant Mindanao. A turn to the west would have meant Japan.

A drizzling rain began falling as I groped my way toward the hatchway, but I didn't go below. The blast of hot, filth-laden air that rushed up from the hold was too much. I lay down in the rain, atop a mound of canvas-covered supplies. I slept in the open every night of the voyage—and was rained on every night.

But there was a compensation and a big one for the discomfort we suffered. The food was the best we had had since the fall of Bataan. Our first breakfast was clean, well-cooked rice with nourishing spinach soup that actually had some spinach in it. At noon dinner there was another mound of rice and a generous-sized dried fish. We stared unbelievingly at the supper fare. In addition to the rice there was a big slab of corned beef.

In the days that followed, the noon meal was augmented by boiled squash or pumpkin soup, to which had been added vitamin B-1 or vitamin B complex. All the water on board had been boiled and made into tea. We had as much of this as we wanted at mealtime and were allowed to fill our canteens twice a day. It was stimulating as well as refreshing.

My body always reacted quickly to the old food treatment and before long I was feeling much better. There was no labor to dissipate the strength we were storing up. We had no illusions, however. The good food was intended to build us up for the labors awaiting us at Davao prison camp.

Not all of us benefited, however. There is always a catch in every decent thing a Jap does. In this case it was the requirement that the Americans form in companies below decks, march up with their mess kits to receive the food, then march down again to eat it in the hold which now was more vile than before because most of the men had been seasick. Some of them, in fact, never were able to retain a meal and were worse off when we eventually docked than when we started. I refused to eat below and always managed to find a perch on top of the junk with which the deck was littered.

After the first day, American officers were ordered to KP duty, to the unconcealed delight of the enlisted men. These "commissioned KPs." soon discovered that the Jap officers had a large store of captured American pork. And though each morsel was a potential case of dysentery, we ate heartily of the generous portions our fellow officers slipped to us. The pork was, of course, a forbidden dish. But if the Japs had been half so observant as they seem to think they are, they could readily have spotted all Americans who had been indulging.

The Japs maintained a sharp lookout day and night—for

what I don't know. The ship was well armed, guns having been mounted fore and aft. Twice during the voyage there was target practice. It came to our attention now that our vessel was in no way marked as a prison ship. It looked like a freighter. If we had been torpedoed by an American or British submarine the death toll would have been appalling, even if we had been given a chance to swim for it.

In addition to the Jap soldiers aboard there were two companies of the old Philippines constabulary which the Japs had renamed the Bureau of Constabulary. They were unwilling passengers, being taken along to fight guerrillas. They were stationed on the port side, forward of the bridge, and opposite the Jap troops.

We learned too late we could have counted on the help of these men had we gone through with a mutiny plot we laid in the early days of the voyage. At that time the talk of taking over the ship was desultory and half-hearted and was confined to the air force officers' group. It was not until we had sailed down through the Sibuyan sea to the port of Iloilo on the island of Panay that our discussions began to take a more serious turn.

There we watched the burial of one of our number who had suffered from seasickness, malaria, and dysentery from the time we left Manila. They put him into a shallow grave beside the wharf and not far from the water's edge. Beyond the dock area we could see a flying field. Two planes were standing on the line, their motors idling. No pilots or ground crew men were near-by. There is nothing we wouldn't have given for a chance at grabbing those planes and taking off. The burial scene reminded us that we too probably were destined to fill nameless graves, far from home.

While we still were in sight of Panay, the fellows got together to size up our chances. We took into our groups a number of marines with whom we had fraternized. Our plan was to strike simultaneously at the engine room, the opening to which was near our quarters; the radio room; and the bridge. The first two would be easily captured, we decided.

The bridge would present greater difficulties. We voted to consult the ranking naval officers on board.

They promptly threw cold water on the scheme. It would be impracticable, they said, because the vessel—an eight-knotter—was too slow and because we would have no place to go. If I had known then the things I now know, we probably would have gone ahead.

I was told later the Filipino constabulary would have attacked the Jap guards at the first hint of encouragement and support. Further, there must have been fifteen or twenty mutiny plots hatching at the same time. Practically every group had one. And there were plenty of places near-by where we would have found haven, had we only known it.

We abandoned the mutiny plan with many regrets. On November 7 our ship tied up at the docks of the Lansang Lumber Company near Davao and we disembarked. Some of the huskier Americans were kept there two days and two nights, working as stevedores on the docks and in the hold of our transport. Most of the prisoners, however, were started marching for Davao prison camp almost immediately. Needless to say, our legs soon began to cramp, because of our long confinement on the ship.

The sun was setting as we started. The brief tropical dusk faded swiftly into darkness. The narrow jungle trail, between high green walls of undergrowth, was illuminated weirdly by the dimmed out headlights on trucks. Mile after mile the corridor wound on, its walls unbroken by crossroads or clearings. They really were putting us away this time. Without complete bush equipment and ample provisions and medicine, no one could hope to live in the jungle that surrounded us.

Men who had been sick aboard ship began falling out soon after the march began. Since they were intended as laborers, however, they were placed in the trucks that moved along with us. But not until Captain Hosume, in charge of the guards, had seen to it they were thoroughly boxed and mauled. Hosume did not approve of the rest periods which were granted nor did he think it right that a water truck had been

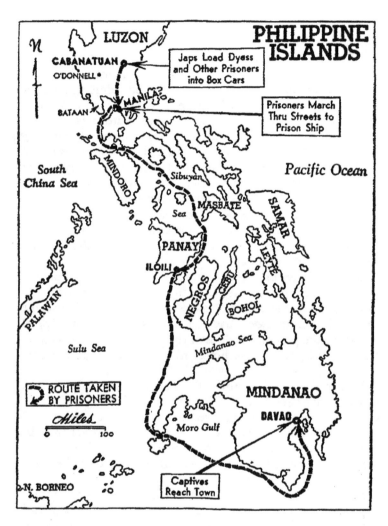

brought along so that we might quench our thirst as often as necessary. These comforts probably were what aroused him to order savage beatings for those who fell out.

We reached the prison about 2 A.M. To our amazement we were fed before being assigned to quarters. They gave us good rice and banana leaf soup. After a few hours' sleep we had a good look at our new home.

Davao had some features in common with O'Donnell and Cabanatuan, but was a permanent establishment. It had been built years before as a penitentiary for offenders against the Philippines commonwealth. More than eighty per cent of its inmates at the time of our arrival were murderers.

Our quarters were within an oblong compound enclosing about ten square acres and barricaded by double walls of barbed wire. In it were eight wooden buildings sixteen feet wide and a hundred feet long. There were watch towers, mounting machine guns; guard stations, machine gun emplacements, and a walking patrol that constantly was on the move outside the barbed wire. Our kitchen was in the compound with the barracks. Just across the road to the east was Japanese headquarters.

In this direction also a railroad paralleled the prison. Eleven kilometers to the south it made junction with the Lansang river. Such outside supplies as were required came up the river from Davao bay on barges and were transshipped by rail to the prison. Produce of the prison shops and plantations went by rail to the junction, then by barge to the port of Davao.

In addition to foodstuffs, the penal colony shipped out sawed lumber and gravel. The railroad ended slightly northeast of the compounds in a sweeping Y, one fork of which led to the stands of timber and the other to the gravel pits. In this general area also were bodegas [warehouses] and other storage centers. The sawmill was directly east of the compounds.

Here also was an old enclosure with guard towers, where Japanese had been interned after the start of the war and before General Sharp's surrender. It now was a hospital area. There was good reason for having a hospital there. The men who worked in the adjacent rice paddies were coming down continually with angry tropical ulcers.

As has been said, a host of diseases are endemic in the Philippines. Any cut or skinbreak develops as a vicious sore

155

within a few hours unless it is cleaned and treated. The Japs' reluctance to make available the proper antiseptics and medications needs no further comment here.

Major Mida, commander of the camp, was displeased when he inspected the American prisoners and saw our emaciated condition. He had asked for laborers, not scarecrows. To our surprise, he did not put the blame on us. Instead, he ordered that we be given rehabilitating food.

In addition to rice, we got pork and beef, cabbage, spinach, squash, onions, potatoes, and peanuts. All these were produced on the camp's vast truck farms and livestock pastures. From the orchards, we had assorted fruit, including bananas to eat raw and plantains, which were baked. There was plenty of water for drinking, bathing, and laundry.

Sick men were sent to the hospital to recuperate. Men more than forty-five years old were not required to work. Guards were tolerant.

It seemed to us at first that in Davao we had found a prison camp very closely approaching heaven. But like most Japanese good things, the swell treatment didn't last. Apparently the recuperation didn't proceed fast enough to please Major Mida; so he took his laborers, anyway, cutting our diet to rice and greens soup. That was enough to sustain life and permit the prisoners to do some work, but no more.

Every man not actually in the hospital was put to work, regardless of age or rank. Chaplains, officers, and enlisted men labored side by side, planting rice, harvesting it in murky paddies, building and cleaning Jap latrines, cultivating crops, and building roads, bridges, and revetments.

The only bright spot was the presence of our friends, the Filipino convicts. They were the grandest bunch of murderers and cutthroats I have ever known. They referred to us as "the gentlemen prisoners." They hated the Japs almost as much as we because the Japs were constantly promising them pardons, asserting that their crimes against the commonwealth were of no concern to Japan.

All they had to do, the Jap authorities told them, was teach the Americans to work hard and very soon they (the Filipinos) would walk out free. But the pardons never came. Consequently, the convicts made it as easy for us as possible. They showed us how to appear very, very busy without actually doing anything. It is amazing how little a Filipino can accomplish if he doesn't want to work. Yet you'd think he was going like sixty. We mastered the trick.

Major Mida may have perceived this, because he transferred most of the Filipino convicts to distant Paulau to work on fortifications. The brunt of the work at Davao then fell upon us.

For two and a half months, I cultivated fields, harvested, cleared jungles, and worked barefoot in the rice paddies. Few of us had shoes. The nails of all my toes still are black from wading in the ooze around Davao.

When Filipinos plant rice they cover their feet and legs with heavy wrappings, but the Japs sent us in barefoot. As we sank knee deep into the bog, our feet and legs were cut by the stones and debris imbedded there. The ulcers followed.

In Jap prison camps virtually all ailments are allowed to run their course, and more often than not the course leads to a shallow grave.

It was not long until my legs were a mass of ulcers. I will carry the scars the rest of my life. Simultaneously, a finger became infected and swelled to triple normal size. For a time it looked as if I might lose it.

To add to my troubles, I fell victim to scurvy, which, with wet and dry beriberi, began sweeping the camp a few weeks after the diet was reduced to rice. It was the old story of vitamin deficiency.

The inside of my mouth was a mass of scurvy blisters so painful that in order to eat I had to throw my head back and drop the rice down in balls, praying none of it would touch the sides or roof of the mouth, My lower lip was swollen and covered with blisters. This came at the same time as my ulcers. The Japs would do nothing for me, though I was very much under the weather.

The scurvy eventually was cured when my friends managed to steal quantities of papaya melons and fruit. The sores healed by themselves.

I have said before that the Japs never seemed to do anything that made sense. Major Mida was crying for laborers, yet he would let men lie sick and inactive when he could have had them on their feet with a little of the fruit that grew in profusion around Davao or by applying a few cents' worth of unguents and antiseptics to their ulcers.

If this was not deliberate cruelty, if it was just the Jap way of doing things, the war probably will be much shorter than we now think. Providing us with fruit, which was rotting on the ground, wouldn't have increased the cost of feeding us. This, I am reliably informed, was less than one cent a man per day.

And, despite our early hopes, it developed that murder and barbarism were to be part of the routine at Davao.

The hospital compound where the sick were kept was the scene of one of several cold-blooded killings that marked our stay at Davao.

An American soldier was one victim. He had been assigned to a task outside the barricade and had been given a pass. He went through the gate and began his duties near the northwest guard tower. After working forty-five minutes he grew thirsty and called to someone within to toss him a canteen of water. A Jap guard in the tower saw the canteen go over the wire. He began shouting and shaking his rifle.

The soldier, believing the guard thought the canteen contained something contraband, unscrewed the top and poured out some of the water to show him it did not. Without a word, the Jap raised his rifle and shot the American three times; once in the chest and twice in the back after he had fallen.

Then in a tantrum, he turned the gun on the hospital building and emptied the magazine. The bullets passed through the pine board structure, but didn't hit any of the patients.

Japanese officers who had witnessed the murder summoned an American surgeon, a lieutenant colonel, who examined the victim and pronounced him dead. The Japs explained to him that the shooting was necessary. The man had tried to escape.

There was nothing we could do in retaliation. Striking a guard or even talking back to him meant almost certain death. I was told by several witnesses of a case on Corregidor in which an American soldier who had been struck by a Jap guard walloped him one in return and knocked him flat.

Another Jap bayoneted him several times from behind. The American died in agony.

Our friends, the Filipino murderers at Davao, took quite a different view of retaliation. They were willing to bide their time, then strike.

One day we were on detail at the edge of the dense Davao jungle with a Filipino—his fellows said he really was a Moro —who a few days before had been tied up and flogged for selling leaf tobacco to an American. He had been brooding and silent for days, and, I came to realize, waiting for his chance.

It came now. The Jap guard called a rest period, then took off his shoes and sat down in the shade of a tree. With a spring so swift it made him look like a little brown blur, the Filipino seized an ax and buried it in the Jap's neck, almost decapitating him. Then he snatched a bolo knife and executed some intricate and pretty shocking carving on the remains.

After this he put on the Jap's shoes, picked up his rifle and, without a glance at us, took to the jungle. We expected terrible repercussions, but as a Filipino convict and not one of us had been responsible, nothing happened.

The aftermath, however, was satisfying—in a creature way —to us. The Japs of Davao turned out en masse for an impressive funeral. After considerable ceremony, the dead man was placed upon a funeral pyre and burned. When the flames had died, ashes were placed in an urn, and the Japs gathered up the beer, rice, meats, sweet cakes, and other foods that had stood near-by during the burning. These they removed to a small building so they would be ready at hand for the departed's spirit when he started his journey to the great beyond.

Well, I guess they had to figure that this was one Jap ghost that 'took his chow with him, because when they went back after it they found only empty beer bottles. There was nothing they could say because, according to Jap tradition, no one but the ghost could have taken the food.

It was the first beer I had had in many a day. And with beef, too!

CHAPTER TWELVE

NEXT TO OUR ESCAPE, the event that will live longest in my memory of Davao prison camp was the arrival around Christmas, 1942, of the Red Cross supplies. No Christmas present I can ever get will thrill me as much.

The Japs pilfered the supplies, robbing us as usual, but what they passed on undoubtedly saved lives. Distribution of the boxes caused the greatest upsurge of spirit and morale in the history of the camp. I saw mature men with tears streaming down their cheeks as they opened their packages.

There were American, British, and South African boxes, all delivered by the International Red Cross. Each man was given a South African box. Then the men, in teams of two, were given an American and a British box to pool between them. There was enough difference to warrant this arrangement. We tossed a coin to decide who would have first choice.

For example, there was tobacco in the American box, but none in the British. On the other hand, the British box contained an extra can of meat.

Other contents included jam, coffee substitute, canned tomatoes, fish, hard biscuit, cheese, prepared puddings, evaporated or condensed milk, instant cocoa, vitaminized essence of orangeade, corned beef, beef and dumplings, tea, sugar, and rice. Among the toilet articles were razors, blades, combs, mirrors, and blessed soap. There also were some knitted sweaters and a few cloth hats.

Despite the first choice scheme we had worked out, we shared the meat, fish, and tobacco. After handing out the boxes, the Japs characteristically shut off the spinach broth they had been giving us with our rice and did not restore it after the supplies were exhausted. This caused more scurvy.

They confiscated a large quantity of bulk cane sugar and chocolate included in the shipment. They told us this would be doled out as we required it. None of it ever was, though they did have a couple of issues of coarse brown sugar which we had produced ourselves.

The thing we resented most was confiscation of the American cigarettes. After my escape, I was able to buy them at four dollars a pack from guerrillas who had penetrated Jap settlements near the prison. Most of them, I suppose, went to Jap soldiers, as did most of the medicines the Red Cross sent.

We had to shrug these things off, of course. Protests would only have brought trouble on the whole camp. To keep our equilibrium we cooked up jokes we would play on the Japs. They seldom tumbled to any of them, but all of us got a kick out of them and felt better about our wrongs.

One of these developed soon after the Filipino killed the Jap guard, whose funeral chow we ate. The word spread that he had been a Moro, not a Filipino, and had joined his people lurking near-by. This alarmed the Japs, who have a mortal fear of Moros. (This fear will be understood by any American soldier who fought through the Philippines campaign of forty-four years ago.)

The Moros are wild, misshapen little men with fiendish faces. And they are deadlier than a cobra. They know the jungle better than anyone.

The Japs never liked the jungle, anyway, and after the guard was killed they appeared to have a horror of it. We utilized the Moro bogey to the full. We did it this way: when a detail was working at the edge of the growth, someone would slip some distance into it and find a hollow log. Upon this he would beat out a booming rhythm with a couple of clubs.

Then someone else would toss a handful of gravel into the brush and the rest of us would yell: "Moros! Moros! Moros!" The Jap guards would turn pale and stare wildly into the dim fastness. Finally, screwing up their courage, they would tiptoe in a few yards, their hands trembling so they couldn't have hit the side of a barn if they had fired.

Having stayed in just long enough to preserve face, they would hurry out again and take the detail to some spot far removed from the jungle. We got easier work this way, too, and they never caught on.

We were even able to turn their "rising sun" ceremony into a joke. About twice a week we had to line up and salute toward the east, the direction of the palace of their Son of Heaven. They always managed to have the Jap flag in the immediate foreground so that to all intents and purposes we were saluting it. We always saluted, but we raised our hands with fingers slightly outspread, allowing the thumb to touch the nose and linger there.

One of our whimsies took a more practical turn. We were continually having to build revetments around the camp. These were supposed to have a solid core of hardwood logs, then be covered with a thickness of clay or other firm earth.

We learned the Japs didn't know a whole lot about various woods, that is, our immediate guards didn't. So we took to building revetments from large stacks of banana and papaya tree trunks, covered with thin layers of earth. A bullet would pass through these as easily as through cardboard. We also learned to string barbed wire entanglements in such a way that a strong pull on a single strand would bring the whole works down like a collapsing tent.

The most fun was when the Japs tried to make plowboys out of a bunch of air force men and marines. I like to remember it because it was the first in a series of events that led to our escape.

The pilots and sea soldiers, who had hung together as a clique, were assigned permanently to the plowing detail and were taken one morning to the coconut grove to get plows and animals. The plows were one-handled, with wooden blades, and belonged in a medieval museum. The animals were humped cattle, resembling the sacred cows of India.

Each had a ring in its nose. Through this a long rope was passed, supposedly for steering the beast. But it couldn't be done. Not by us, anyway. The cows responded in two ways to our steering: they would (1) balk or (2) apparently conclude the plowman was daffy and go bellowing and charging around the patch ripping up the soil and even wrecking adjoining patches of growing stuff.

I am a country boy and have chopped and picked cotton, hoed corn, and tended truck patches, but I never learned to plow. The only man there who ever had was a graduate of Texas A. & M. college. He commented:

"Man and boy, I plowed with stubborn Texas mules, but all my experience with them is no help with these misborn dromedaries!"

There was no use cussing them in English, because they didn't understand it. Well, we would go tearing around, the Americans swearing at the cattle, the Japs swearing at the Americans, and the cattle bellowing at both the Americans and the Japs. After a day's plowing, the field looked as if it had been dive-bombed, strafed, and had been fought over by tanks in a major engagement.

Finally the rains came, settling the terrain and showing that the field was full of great, barren islands of untouched hard ground. As punishment, the Japs made us sit around during the rainy season doing minor jobs in the swamp. I came down with malaria and a skin infection at the same time. Ailments always went in pairs for me.

It was in the midst of my disabilities that the Japs decided to let us have a Christmas celebration. We never were able to figure out why. Major Mida announced there would be no

163

work of any kind. On Christmas morning we were assembled in the open ground beside our barracks and were greeted by a large group of Filipino civilians who lived in the region. They filed among us, handing out little holiday cakes made of cassava root and molasses. Each was wrapped in a banana leaf. They were delicious.

After we had eaten, we sang Christmas carols and other songs, the Filipinos joining in as best they could. In the afternoon there was a more formal entertainment, but the Japs ruined it by horning in. The Filipino youngsters did native dances and we sang; solos, quartets, and all together. Then the Japs got into the spirit of the thing and insisted on singing some war songs. It was the awfulest caterwauling I ever have listened to. The howling was followed by sword dances which were accompanied by ear-splitting whoops and yells. My aches and pains kept me from enjoying the good parts of the show and the Japs' contributions almost drove me out of my head.

I kept up my strength during the malaria siege, thanks to extra grub which was spirited out of the kitchen for me by Sam Grashio, who was assigned there. This bridged me over until receipt of some quinine from the International Red Cross. The Japs issued enough of this to knock the fever.

When I recovered, late in January, 1943, there was another development in the escape pattern. A Jap noncom was sent around to tell me that because of my skill with the cattle, I had been chosen to drive the camp bull cart as a permanent assignment. I looked at him sharply, but he wasn't kidding. So I entered into my role as bull driver.

The cart was used to haul coffee and other produce from the plantation to the bodega. It carried implements and supplies to the work details and performed a sort of general errand service throughout the camp.

At first, the cart was inspected thoroughly at all guard outposts, going and coming. As the guards got to know me one or two even showed faint signs of friendliness and grew lax in their inspections.

I did all I could to help this spirit along. Hopes of escape, which never had been entirely absent during my imprisonment, were beginning to rise. The vague outlines of a plan were forming in my mind as I plodded along beside the bulls. To the guards I now was "very good." This is one of three expressions every Jap knows. The others are "okay" and "no good." It was about this time that I got another chance to widen my circle of friends. The Jap authorities instituted English classes and I became one of the teachers. The guards were issued Japanese-English dictionaries. We made some progress, though these lessons were harder on the instructors than on the pupils. Japanese is a terrible language to learn or teach—especially teach. The first thing the guards wanted to know, of course, were "cursing" words. There was one fellow whom we called "Betty Boop" because of his plump cheeks, who grew quite proud of the word I taught him. He caused me much embarrassment afterward.

Whenever he saw me, no matter at what distance, he would yell out this word at the top of his lungs. It caused much merriment among the Americans, and I think it brought me some good will among the Japs. It was the nearest we ever came to good-natured kidding with our captors.

We had names for all the Jap guards, usually based on their physical characteristics. Because of his big ears, we named one "Clark Gable." The biggest, blackest, and stupidest Jap I have ever seen was, of course, dubbed "Big Stoop," from Milt Caniff's comic strip, "Terry and the Pirates."

"Robert Taylor" was, I must say, genuinely handsome, and we found he was a sucker for flattery. He would stride up and down with his chest out and let us feel his muscles. He became so vain that he started changing his uniform every three or four weeks, a practice almost unheard of among the Japs.

The English classes, however, deprived us of one of our favorite diversions. It had been our happy custom to smile upon our Jap guards and call them everything under the sun, beginning with their ancestry and coming on down. This now had to stop. They were getting to know too many words.

Meanwhile, I had other things to think about. I had pretty

well established myself as the camp's No. 1 good will ambassador. I figured it was time to begin cashing in.

It was now along in February and the outline of a plan for escape no longer was vague in my mind. I remember the time, because it was then we were allowed to send postal cards home. My spirits had so risen that I added four words to my message: "I will be home."

Having done that, I determined to lay some groundwork for the actual attempt. I did so that night.

Thoughts of escape from the Japs were by no means new to me or to any other prisoners. We had entertained them at O'Donnell and Cabanatuan camps, on the prison ship, and here at Davao. The odds always had been hopeless. But now, I was ready to try to make up a party.

It was a night in February, 1943, that I sat down on a bunk in the rear of the barracks beside Captain (now Major) Austin C. Shofner, of the U. S. Marines, whom we called "Shifty." We were well removed from the others in the long, bleak room. We talked more than an hour and decided to sleep on it.

It still looked good the next night, and we decided to give it a try even if we lost our lives. We discussed the men about us as possible companions. Shifty suggested two marine captains, now majors. They are Majs. Jack Hawkins and Michael Dobervitch, both fearless, resourceful, dependable, and in fair physical condition. Jack, a naval academy graduate, remembered something of his navigation and spoke Spanish as well. Mike was powerfully built and a bull for work.

I mentioned Sam Grashio and Leo. Sam had given up his job in the kitchen because he hated the Japs so much he could no longer trust himself in a spot where butcher knives were at hand. Leo was one of the finest airplane engineers and motor experts I have ever known. He was employed in the machine shop.

[*Editor's note: Colonel Dyess employs only a given name where there is uncertainty that the man has as yet reached the continental United States.*]

The next day, while Shifty was feeling out the marines, I

walked up to Sam and asked him if he'd like to go over the hill with me. He replied at once:

"When do we go? Right now? Sure!"

Leo and I had talked about escape many times, but the difficulties of equipment and assembling the right sort of party always were too great. Leo was one of the men who had escaped Cabcaben field, but had failed to reach Australia.

I told him I thought the time now was right. He said heartily that he still was all for it. We talked it over at length, and Leo said he could make fishhooks, knives, and other jungle equipment. I saw Shifty soon afterward. He reported Mike and Jack were rarin' to go. That night the six of us met in the darkness behind the barracks.

We agreed to begin active preparations the next day, holding out bits of food at meal time and secreting any weapons or tools we could find. There was quite a list of things we would need before launching our effort.

These included food, leggings as a protection against insects and scratches from thorns and undergrowth, quinine for malaria, antiseptics and other medicines for treating scratches to head off tropical ulcers, shoes, blankets, or shelter tent halves, mosquito bars, matches, small knives or daggers and bolo knives for hacking our day through the growth, a watch, compass, sextant, and—by no means least—money.

All were vital. And we had only clothes, shoes, and blankets. After several more of our nightly talks, we concluded we would need an expert navigator, as we envisioned a long voyage in a boat of some sort and Jack didn't think he remembered enough navigation for such an undertaking.

We talked over the available naval personnel and eventually agreed upon Lieutenant Commander (now Commander) Melvyn H. McCoy. He had been captured on Corregidor, and I had first met him at Cabanatuan prison camp. When Shifty propositioned him, McCoy was enthusiastic, but said he would have to bring along three men associated with him on the coffee picking detail, which McCoy directed.

These were Major Stephen M. Mellnik of the coast artillery, and two army enlisted men, Paul and Bob. McCoy and his men were able to make a real contribution. Their coffee plantation was near the poultry farm and they began swiping chickens, which we traded for such nonperishable food as tinned or dried fish, hard biscuits, and other items.

Leo meanwhile was busy. He held out some of the bolos that came his way, cutting them down to dagger size, or preserving them intact. His crowning achievement was fashioning a crude sextant that actually worked.

We stole a watch and compass from the Japs, but we didn't feel bad about the watch, for it once had belonged to an American soldier. We picked up the maps here and there.

And during the weeks these details were being arranged we got two Filipino recruits, Ben and Victor. Sam enlisted Ben, who recommended Victor because of his knowledge of jungle craft.

It should be made clear that each time an intimation of our plan was imparted to an outsider we ran a terrible risk. One did not have to escape or even attempt to escape to bring down upon himself and comrades the most appalling of punishments. We all knew the story of the American soldier and his Filipino friend who planned a break from the Negros Island camp. They told their plans to one person too many and the Japs found their little store of supplies. This evidence of intended escape resulted in the summary beheadal of both men.

After Ben and Victor had been admitted to the plot, we decided they would be the last. We told no other prisoners our plans.

This was partially for their own protection. If, after the escape, the Japs should suspect any remaining prisoner of having advance knowledge of it, that individual's head would be as good as rolling in the sand.

We also determined to kill no Japs in our escape, for this would bring reprisals upon the entire camp. We therefore had to lay our plans much more carefully.

There were two courses: (1) to escape from the compound at night, and this would be virtually impossible, or (2) to break away from a detail, but this might entail knocking out

168

a guard and also would cause reprisals. We decided we would have to figure some other way; something involving a slip-away. We did, later.

The Ides of March came and passed. With the exception of a few trifles and extras, we had all our equipment. There was only the problem of caching it at the spot in the jungle from which we intended to take off, but what a problem!

Some of the things were in the possession of individual men. Others were at the appointed place. But the bulk of the stuff was on the opposite side of the camp.

As the time drew near, we knew we must act. That is where the bull cart and friendly guards came in. I had been hauling poles for fences. A few days later, during the noon hour ebb, I drove to the coffee detail where Mellnik, McCoy, Paul, and Bob had prepared a load of poles similar to those I had been transporting. This was near the jungle edge where our supplies lay.

We put the supplies into the bed of the cart and laid the poles over them. Mellnik sat atop the load, supposedly to make certain no poles fell off. I walked, driving the bulls.

I followed a feeder road leading into a secondary road which cut directly across the middle of the camp to the place where the fence detail had been working at the fringe of the jungle. All along the way we met Jap guards, but they either paid no attention or grunted a greeting. We passed beneath tower watchers and in front of machine gun emplacements.

I was on pins and needles, not because we were doing anything unusual, but because the individual Jap is unpredictable. We were sure all was well, but you can never tell when you're dealing with Japs.

We were dismayed to find a Jap guard posted just a few yards up the road from our destination. I didn't know him. He turned and looked at us. Well, there was nothing to do but start unloading. Any funny business then would have been fatal. We began hauling the poles off the cart. The Jap watched a minute, then turned his head.

The poles came off on his side and the supplies went off on the opposite side and into the tall jungle grass. They would

169

get soaking wet, for the rains were coming down every day, but that couldn't be helped.

That night, as we Americans shook hands in the darkness behind the barracks, we felt the worst was over. We decided it now was time to set a date and complete our plans.

Most of us thought that a Sunday would be the time, because there would be only a few details sent out and vigilance would be relaxed. Sunday details usually performed minor tasks near the barricades and no Jap guards went along. There was a shortage of them, and this was their day of rest.

On Saturday night, March 27, 1943, we were ready and determined to make our break the next day. Somehow, however, I felt something was wrong, I couldn't say what. I just didn't believe we were going. I was sure something would happen. That's how psychic you get in a prison camp. We didn't go. The Japs ordered all hands out—with guards—to plant rice.

We were delayed a week, but we used that week well. We observed the tower guards and the patrol. We timed our movements. We measured distances. And at midweek we learned the attempt would have to be made the following Sunday or not at all.

Reinforcements were coming. There would be guards with the details on Sundays as well as other days. Sunday, April 4, would be the last day prisoners would go outside alone. It was time for final plans.

CHAPTER THIRTEEN

On SATURDAY NIGHT, April 3, we gave our plans a final going over. We satisfied ourselves that if the venture should end in disaster, it would not be because of any bungle on our part. We had committed to memory the route, the timing, and how we would conduct ourselves. There were plenty of long chances ahead, but we had to take them, trusting in God.

The ten Americans were to get out of the compound by means of a slight hocus-pocus in connection with the day's work details. The two Filipinos, being prisoners of the commonwealth, could get away easily enough from the convicts' compound after the routine Sunday morning count. The two details and the Filipinos would rendezvous according to the plan already worked out.

Sunday morning dawned bright and clear. We were up early. Our men finished breakfast, then drew the regulation rations issued to details that are to work outside the barricade. Each man got a mess kit filled with rice. There were two large tin cans of soup to be heated at chow time. There was some additional equipment that had been accumulated at the last minute, and this we distributed about our persons.

Shifty led the first detail, which was made up of Jack, Mike, and Sam. McCoy led the second detail, made up of Mellnik, Paul, Bob, Leo, and myself.

The first group fell in and marched to the southeast gate, through which it was passed without question, and proceeded straight east, crossing the main road and the tracks. Within a few minutes, the first four men were at the rendezvous.

Now it was our turn. I have spoken before of the prayers, silent prayers, we used to say at O'Donnell and Cabanatuan camps and of how I came to think of God as a man thinks of his commanding officer—as "The Old Man." I knew that the next minute or two would bring the supreme test for us.

I didn't exactly pray, but I thought to myself: "If the Old Man is with us, we'll make it. If He isn't, we won't."

We halted at the gate. McCoy, whom the guards had seen as a detail leader in the past, stepped up and saluted.

One of the Japs stepped out into the road to look us over closely. Whether he actually was more suspicious than usual I don't know, but he did hesitate. Usually the guard made a swift count, then called it off to one of his partners, who would chalk it on a board.

This fellow, however, continued to stand and look at us. There was plenty of chance for a slip. Even a cursory examination of our persons would have disclosed enough contraband to have lost all of us our heads. It seemed to me that I clanked when I walked.

It was a long moment. Then suddenly the guard snapped: "O.K.!" and stepped back. His partner chalked us down. We passed through the gate.

We were in plain view of guards with binoculars on the northwest and southwest towers of the camp.

We walked as nonchalantly as possible, but it seemed to me that my heart was beating my brains out. I thought I could actually feel the guards' eyes on the back of my neck.

As we crossed a road one at a time, we were so close a guard could easily have knocked us off with his gun. Obviously he didn't notice us. There was no outcry.

When we were all across, I thought to myself: "The Old Man *is* with us today. What we're having is more than luck; a lot more than luck."

Skirting the southern boundary of the hospital and chapel compounds, we crossed a wide open space and neared the main road, which was to be our greatest hazard. A guard was stationed there, about twenty yards from where we were to cross.

It had been our intention to slip across, one by one, but as we were about to do so we saw a Filipino, whom we did not know, coming down the road between us and the guard. He saw us. There was only one thing to do.

Snapping into detail formation, we walked boldly across, looking neither right nor left. The Filipino said nothing. We stepped into the tall grass on the opposite side and kept going.

If the guard had shouted or fired, he would have attracted the attention of a second Jap on a smaller road to the east and a large Jap outpost farther south. An outcry would have brought the entire camp down upon us.

The last bad place was just ahead—the small road to the east. We crept up and waited at its edge. Watching our chance, we infiltrated across, one by one, using the tactics some of us had learned when we fought as infantry on Bataan. We now were in the banana plantation, through which we moved northward, passing Jap headquarters almost hidden in the trees.

We continued through the thick foliage until we reached our cached supplies. As expected, they were soaked. We wrung them out, slung them across our backs, and in a few steps reached the rendezvous. Shofner and the others were waiting. We made an equitable distribution of the equipment. We now had only to wait for Ben and Victor and we would be on our way.

We stood silently in the jungle fastness. We could hear nothing. It seemed like an hour that we waited, keenly conscious that every minute we lost was a minute gained for the Japs—and they would be able to travel much faster than we because of our weakened condition. I wondered if the two Filipinos could have given us away in the hope of speeding the pardons promised them by the Japs.

Then, like a wraith, Victor materialized out of the jungle. He whispered that Ben was waiting a short distance off, that he would fetch him. Waiting, I stood silent in the dim twilight of matted vines and trees. Then I heard someone coming noisily. I drew my fighting bolo. Presently, I could see a Filipino, a stranger, making his way along. He passed within three and a half feet of me and disappeared. Then we heard the blows of his bolo as he chopped at trees.

It was about now that the daily rain started coming down. From his place of concealment, Leo whispered: "Good old rain. It'll cover our tracks."

"Cover our tracks, hell!" said Shifty. "I wish those guys would come on so we could start making some tracks."

Ben and Victor appeared shortly afterward. They explained that on leaving the compound they had met some Filipinos they didn't trust and had to linger to allay suspicion. They were just about thirty minutes late.

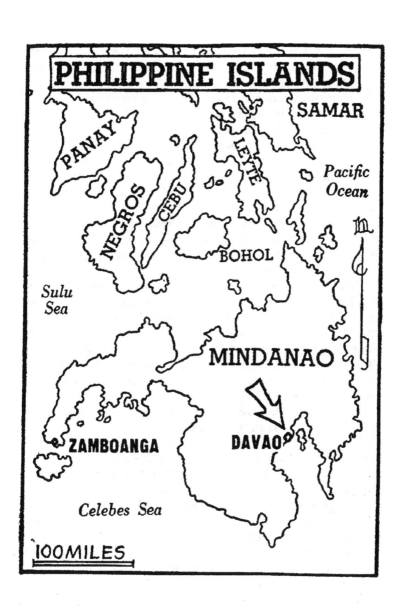

PHILIPPINE ISLANDS

SAMAR

PANAY

LEYTE

NEGROS

CEBU

Pacific
Ocean

BOHOL

Sulu
Sea

MINDANAO

ZAMBOANGA

DAVAO

Celebes Sea

100MILES

At 10:15 A.M. we plunged into the dense Davao jungle, strung out in single file, Victor in the lead. One man hung to the rear to give the alarm in the event we were pursued. The rain continud to come down. The ooze was knee deep and the dim path often dipped through water-filled gullies. There were mosquitoes by the millions.

The going almost immediately grew more difficult. It was necessary to slash a path through the undergrowth. Once the Japs found this trail, they would be up with us in no time.

Our course led across many jungle streams, swollen by the rains. Some were too deep to wade and we had to chop down trees to use as bridges. Someone had brought some rope, which proved invaluable in crossing the water hazards. Because our strength was not up to par, we quickly grew weary. The rain-soaked packs got heavier and heavier.

About thirty minutes before dark, we halted. We had drunk all our water, and as we could not drink jungle water we had to find another supply. Victor knew the answer to this. He pulled down some buhuka, the serpentine, straggling vines that grow among the trees, and snipped off the ends. (The water contained in these hollow stems has been purified by vegetable action. The end is held in the mouth and the water trickles down.)

We pushed on a little farther that night, then came to the bank of a stream so swollen we didn't want to tackle it in the darkness. We cut down trees and from the trunks and smaller branches built four raised beds to keep us above the water. We ate the rice issued to us that morning. It had soured during the day. Then we tried to sleep. We felt fairly secure, knowing the Japs would be unable to find us that night.

The rain had stopped. The jungle grew weirdly silent. We could hear only the bubbling of water in the stream and the whine of dive bomber mosquitoes. We were dozing when there was a resounding crash followed by heavy splashes and some of the most spectacular profanity I ever have listened to. The marines' bed had collapsed, dropping them into the water and ooze.

Shifty was the only one of us who didn't sleep that night.

He insisted he could hear jungle drums, booming intermittently during the dark hours. I won't say he didn't. I came to know in the days ahead that you can hear anything in the jungle.

Daylight of the second day showed us that the stream barring our progress had risen during the night. We cut nearly a dozen trees to bridge it. Going was much more difficult after we reached the other side.

Our Filipino comrades, Victor and Ben, went ahead, swinging their razor-sharp bolos at the matted growth. Jack walked immediately behind them with the compass. At first we checked the course every fifteen or twenty minutes, but we soon found we were zigzagging and losing time, so we started checking it every four to five minutes.

The buhuka vine, which had quenched our thirst the day before, now seemed to regret its helpfulness and became a painful hindrance. Its fibrous covering is studded with thorns, which tore our clothing and us.

We came to places in the jungle impossible to cut through. Sometimes we climbed over, and again we crawled under, holding our noses just above the slime and expecting to meet snakes face to face.

At 9 A.M. we checked our progress and found we had been making even poorer time than we had thought. This was dangerous. Once the Japs picked up our broad trail, they would have the benefit of our clearance work and would travel much faster than we.

At 10 A.M. the jungle ended and we were in the great swamp. The water was knee deep with soft mud at the bottom. There were occasional grassy hummocks of firm ground, but not enough of them to help us much. Sword grass grew ten and twelve feet high. Every time a blade of it struck us it laid the skin open like a knife. Victor and Ben wrapped their hands and faces, but they were bleeding profusely in a short time.

The heat was steamy and weakening. We were soaked with sweat. We had passed up breakfast to conserve our meager supply of food.

We made even less progress as the sword grass grew thicker and more robust. There was nothing to do but go on. Only the prison lay behind and we knew we'd have to cross the swamp somewhere. Often, after cutting twenty-five yards or so, we encountered clumps that were too much even for the keen bolos. We would have to retreat and try again. It was not uncommon to make less than a hundred yards in an hour. At 2 P.M. we were about finished.

Heat, hunger, fatigue, and the difficult going were almost too much. We remembered having passed an enormous log about thirty feet long which rested near a large fallen tree. It took almost an hour to get back to it. Every time I threw myself down on a grassy hummock to rest I would look at the dark water and think, "Oh, what the hell! Why not just stay here?"

When we reached the log, we opened a can of meat filched from the Japs. This gave us strength to gather dry twigs which Victor used to build a fire on the broader end of the log. While he cooked rice in one bucket and made tea in the other, we cut trees to form the framework of our beds for the night.

We were in the midst of this when Leo shouted: "Duck! Duck!" An angry humming filled the air. Then we saw what seemed to be thousands of bees. They were the biggest brutes I ever saw. Their hive must have been in the log near the spot where Victor built the fire. When two of them hit me in the back simultaneously, I thought I had been stabbed.

I fell forward across the log and covered my head with my hands. About a dozen bees had a try at me as I found later when I picked their stingers out of my shirt. Bob was stung a dozen times before he plunged into the water. No one escaped. The bees raised hell more than half an hour, then left us.

The pain of the stings took our minds temporarily off our other troubles, and we proceeded rapidly with the business of building our platform. When it was ready, the rice and tea were waiting. As we ate we discussed strategy.

Everyone wanted to go ahead, but we had no way of knowing how much swamp remained to be conquered. Our shoes were falling apart. Our legs and bodies had been slashed severely by the sword grass. Infections would start swiftly. Another day like this one would finish us off, we thought.

An eerie glow appeared in the west. Some of us thought it might be a forest fire, but it was obvious that if this were true the fire must be many miles off. Then we saw that the east was glowing also and realized we were seeing one of those strange tropical sunsets that lights up the sky in all directions.

We hung our wet shoes on poles and rigged our mosquito bars as best we could. We got out our blankets and shelter tent halves. All this time we were talking in low voices, just loud enough to be heard above the noises of the swamp.

Settling down to rest I found a depression between two tree trunks and made myself fairly comfortable. I was exhausted. But before dropping off to sleep I got to thinking of the odds against me.

Sam was lying on one side of me and Shifty on the other. I don't know what made me do it, but on the impulse I turned to Shifty and said.

"Don't you think Sam ought to lead us in a little prayer?"

There had been a lot of silent prayer among us during the last three days. I am sure of that, though I can speak only for myself. Sam was the most religious boy in the bunch. He was of Italian ancestry and was a Catholic, having been an altar boy when he was a kid.

Sam was a quiet sort of youngster, slight of build and slender. Unlike many persons of Italian blood he had blond hair. He had spent some years as an amateur boxer and in some bout or other his nose had been flattened slightly. Shifty answered my question at once.

"I sure do think he ought to, Ed," he said.

"How about it, Sam?" I asked.

"All right," he said. "Let's all start off with the Lord's Prayer."

We said the Lord's Prayer with Sam leading us and some of the boys stumbling over the words. Then Sam continued on alone with something that sounded like one of the Cath-

olic litanies, but none of us knew any responses. He finishe
with a prayer that was based partially on one of the psalm:
but most of it was his own.

In this he asked God to deliver us from our enemies, t
protect us from disease and the jungle, to deliver us out o
the swamp, and to see us safely into the American lines. H
concluded:

"We ask it in Your name. Amen." We all echoed "Amen.'
I felt easier and more optimistic than I had since the star
of the escape. The next minute I was dead to the world.
There was only one interruption during the night. Two of
the marines fell through their bed and into the water.

At daylight we were up for our third day in the jungle.
Victor made tea and cooked some of the dwindling supply of
rice.

We decided to continue through the swamp. We felt better
after our sleep and the stimulation of rice and tea. At 8 A.M.
we were slashing away again. The first two hours took us
through the toughest part of the great morass.

At 10 A.M. the sword grass grew thinner and the water shal-
lower. It was still tough going, make no mistake about that,
and the heat again had grown steamy, stifling, and enervat-
ing. But we were much encouraged.

Then, at 2 P.M., the swamp ended as abruptly as it had
begun and we stepped into the gloom and slime of the jungle.
It was almost as good as getting back home, though this part
of the jungle presented difficulties all its own. There were
scores of leeches which burrowed into the skin at every un-
protected place.

It was a mistake to pull them off, because the heads remained under the skin and continued to burrow, eventually
causing great sores. The only remedy was to burn them off
or rub tobacco into the sores.

After an hour of splashing along we struck a dim trail that
seemed to lead in the general direction we wanted.

We had gone only a little way when there was an exclama-
tion from one of the fellows. He had stopped and was staring

down. In the mold were footprints. Most of them had been made by split-toed shoes with hobnail heels.

This could mean only one thing—Jap soldiers! The split-toed shoes give the feet more freedom on difficult terrain and assist the wearer in climbing trees for sniping. But the thing that jarred us was that the prints were fresh.

We dashed into the cover of the jungle and conferred. Victor, Ben, and Bob then scouted north, while Shifty and Leo watched in our immediate vicinity. The rest of us went on to a clearing where the sun beat down, and there we spread out our equipment to dry.

At 5:30 P.M. the scouts returned, reporting they had found signs of heavy foot traffic and a group of newly deserted houses. There were prints obviously made by Filipinos.

They brought back some native sweet potatoes and plantains that could be tossed into the coals and baked. We began chopping down trees to build bunks for the night. We remained cautious, however.

Despite the progress we had made during the day we spent a miserable night. Being back in the jungle, we were vulnerable again to those dive-bombing mosquitoes. I slept almost not at all. The one time I was about to drop off there was a ripping crash, followed by bitter profanity.

The marines' bed had collapsed—as usual.

CHAPTER FOURTEEN

THE DAYS THAT FOLLOWED were much alike: a succession of jungle, swamp, mountains, swollen rivers, and rain. The rough going was beginning to tell on our weakened bodies.

There was little medicine left in our waterproof bag. There

were no antiseptics for treating the tropical ulcers which had developed as infections from scratches and abrasions which were unavoidable in this wild and brush-covered country. We seemed to take turns being sick. This was fortunate because there always was someone well enough to rally the others.

And it was important that we rally because we still were within reach of the enemy. I can't tell you anything about our destination, except that we had one. At times it seemed very far off and almost unattainable, but all of us were spurred toward it by our memories of O'Donnell camp, Cabanatuan, and Davao.

We always were able to thank God we were anywhere except back among the Japs, subject to their barbaric cruelties, their policy of systematic starvation, and their creed of murder for captives. Even when things were at their worst we could say to ourselves that we were damn well off.

We occasionally encountered tribes of natives.

Many of the amazing adventures, ludicrous and serious mishaps, and aimless wanderings that marked that journey of ours are contained in my diary. Someday, when our lost possessions in the Pacific are regained, all these things may be published.

There is one story I can tell in full, however, and I don't think I can tell it too often. It has to do with the faith we placed in God and His response to our prayers. There was much silent prayer among us all through our ordeal, but there were times also when we prayed aloud, led by Sam Grashio.

Sam's prayers were so straightforward we had to believe with him that God was listening. Just as I always thought of God as "The Old Man"—in the sense of a commanding officer—Sam ran in many homely expressions in the brief prayers that usually began and ended with the Lord's Prayer. These made us feel that we were talking directly to God—man to man. One of these passages I remember particularly well.

"Lord," Sam would say, "pickin's are bum for us, as You

know. But we know You are going to see to it that they get better."

One day, long, long afterward, and many a mile from the scene of our trials, we were to remember those prayers with a guilty start. It was a gala occasion and several of us, full of wine and food, were joking about some of the things we had been through. Sam walked in. I thought he looked a little disapproving. But he grinned and walked up to the table. What he said was said in a kidding way, though I have always thought he was about two-thirds serious.

"Look at you!" Sam said. "Just look at you. When pickin's were bum you begged old Sam to pray for you. But now pickin's are good, what do you do? You gorge your bellies and fill up on wine and forget all about old Sam and God, too."

You can call that speech what you want to. I call it a powerful sermon. If it did nothing else, it reminded me that days had passed since I had thanked God for my deliverance.

Our journey through Mindanao ended almost as suddenly as it had begun. We reached our objective and enjoyed blessed relief. We had to wait many days for orders and assignments and when physical recovery was under way we began to fret at the delay. The food was scanty, and the flies descended upon us by the millions. A diary entry for one of those days reads:

"Very little food in this fly-bitten place. There is nothing worse than waiting. [Three members of the party] went out to search for food and didn't return. A little worried about them."

The next day's entry is one brief line: "[The party] returned."

Within a few hours after that was written we got our orders. They brought with them a thrill that blotted out the misery of the past. We were fighting men once more!

CPSIA information can be obtained
at www.ICGtesting.com
Printed in the USA
BVHW081841271021
620048BV00002B/19